W9-AAD-093

Who's Rocking the Cradle?
Women Pioneers of Oklahoma Politics
From Socialism to the KKK
1900–1930

Suzanne H. Schrems, Ph.D.

HORSE CREEK PUBLICATIONS, INC.

Norman, Oklahoma
www.HorseCreekPublications.com

Who's Rocking the Cradle? Women Pioneers of Oklahoma Politics from Socialism to the KKK, 1900–1930
Copyright (c) 2004 Horse Creek Publications, Inc.
First Printing 2004
Manufactured in the United States of America

All rights reserved. No part of this book may be reproduced or transmitted in any form or by any means, electronic or mechanical, including photocopying, recording, or by any information storage and retrieval system, without permission in writing from the author, except by a reviewer who may quote brief passages in a review.

Cover design: Edward L. Schrems, Norman, Oklahoma
Copy Editing: Andrea Howe, Blue Falcon Editing. www.bluefalconediting.com
Front cover picture derived from: *Election Day*, a cartoon by E. W. Gustin 1909. Library of Congress, Prints and Photographs Division, LC-USZ62-51821 DLC

Library of Congress Cataloging-in-Publication Data

Schrems, Suzanne H.
  Who's rocking the cradle? : women pioneers of Oklahoma politics from socialism to the KKK, 1900-1930 / Suzanne H. Schrems.
      p. cm.
  Includes bibliographical references and index.
  ISBN 0-9722217-2-7 (pbk.)
  1. Women in politics--Oklahoma--History--20th century. 2. Oklahoma--Politics and government--20th century. I. Title.
  HQ1236.5.U6S36 2004
  320'.082'09766--dc22
                              2004005166

Contents

*Dedicated to
Courtney Johnson, Raegan Johnson,
and Eleanor Schrems*

Preface

This study began with my interest in the political culture of conservative women. Before I began, I was aware that most political studies emphasized the fight of feminists for the passage of the Susan B. Anthony Suffrage Amendment in the federal constitution, and later, the fight of women in the National Woman's party for an equal rights amendment. For the most part, however, these studies do not address the motivations of conservative women, many of whom fought against woman suffrage, to enter the political arena. My curiosity about women's political culture led me to the archives at the University of Oklahoma where I found an abundance of sources that tell the history of Oklahoma women's political culture in the early twentieth century, especially after receiving the right to vote in Oklahoma in 1918. I drew on these materials to tell a history that illustrated the political activities of women on the left of the political spectrum as well as those on the right.

My purposes in writing this study are twofold. First, publication of this research adds to the historiography of women in politics by including conservative women in the discussion of women's political cultural in the early twentieth century. Second, a discussion of the roots of women's political philosophy helps us to understand many of the positions that divide women today, and provides an understanding of the different political philosophies held by twenty-first century women. One of the things that struck me most during my research was how little the argument has changed since the early twentieth century. The ideological alignment still seems to be over the role of the state in solving societal problems. And, as in the early twentieth century, today's women align themselves at different positions on the ideological spectrum.

One of the pleasures in doing this research was having access to the numerous source materials found in state and university archives. John

Lovett, Assistant Curator at the Western History Collection, University of Oklahoma, allowed me to copy the "Oklahoma Women in Politics" column in *Harlow's Weekly*. There was a mountain of information in the column about the political activities of Oklahoma women before and after suffrage. Without being able to refer to the column, this study would have been very difficult. It was, and is, a pleasure to do research in the Western History Collection. Not only is the professional staff helpful, but the atmosphere is conducive to the long hours spent looking through file folders and old newspaper clippings in the numerous collections that house information on Oklahoma women in politics.

Two people in particular stand out as very helpful in gathering information and putting this manuscript together. First is my long time friend, Cindy Wolff, Director of the Department of Labor Library in Washington, D.C., who helped me do research at various government archives. I also appreciate the editorial guidance of Dallas Schrems, who read through each chapter and corrected my awkward prose and numerous typos and grammatical errors. Lastly, I am so very thankful for the cooperation of little Eleanor Schrems, an infant in my charge who slept ever so peacefully day after day as I typed away in my office. To her and to Courtney and Raegan Johnson this book is dedicated.

The Roots of Political Activism

Francis Willard, national president of the Women's Christian Temperance Union (WCTU) in 1888, stressed the importance of women assuming a role in politics in order to spread to all of society the values and virtues they maintained in their homes. It was women's mission "to make the whole world home like," Willard lectured, and to "come into government and purify it, into politics and cleanse its stygian pool, for woman will make home-like every place on this round earth."[1] The WCTU was one of the first organizations to promote women's political equality in Oklahoma. In 1888 Willard visited Indian Territory, in present-day eastern Oklahoma, to encourage women to organize branches or "Unions" in their districts so that western women could influence the social and moral fiber of frontier communities and take an active role in public life.[2] It was one of the chief goals of the WCTU to involve women in the legislative process and the governance of the nation's laws. A resolution passed by the organization explained, "much of the evil by which this country is cursed comes from the fact that men in power whose duty it is to make and administer the laws had failed."[3]

The growth of the WCTU in the American West encouraged women in the National American Woman Suffrage Association (NAWSA) to expand their campaign westward. In 1895 the NAWSA sent organizers into Indian and Oklahoma Territories to establish regional offices. The ladies immediately went to work gathering support for suffrage and, by the end of the year, sent their first suffrage bill to the legislature. The lawmakers evidently were not receptive to giving women political equality; the resolution did not pass, and subsequently the movement lost momentum until 1904. In that year the national suffrage office sent Laura Gregg from Kansas to organize in the Twin Territories. Gregg spent eight months speaking and recruiting women into the NAWSA. With the organization

I

of the Territories into the state of Oklahoma in 1907, women stepped up their campaign to influence constitutional delegates to include woman suffrage in the new state constitution.[4] Susan B. Anthony, the leading suffrage activist, warned that "no stone should be left unturned to secure suffrage for the women while Oklahoma is yet a Territory, for if it comes into the Union without this in its constitution it will take a long time and a great deal of work to convert over one-half of the men to vote for it."[5]

To rally support for woman suffrage in the state, Oklahoma women joined with national suffragists on a speaking tour of patriotic groups such as the Grand Army of the Republic, at teachers' institutes, business colleges, country schoolhouse meetings, and women's clubs. The suffragists also rode in holiday parades and appeared at county fairs. By so doing, the women brought attention to their cause and inspired many organizations to pass resolutions supporting woman suffrage.[6] When the constitutional convention convened at Guthrie in 1907, suffragists opened an office in the territorial capital to provide a coordinated effort to bring the issue of woman suffrage to the convention floor. Many attempts were made to silence the women, but eventually the suffrage proposal made it to the floor for debate. Suffrage proponents among the delegates, such as labor leader Pete Hanraty and future Oklahoma Senator Robert Owen, fought hard for suffrage but ultimately could not stem the apparent animus held by most delegates regarding women's political equality. After the long and heated debate, delegates voted down the suffrage resolution.[7]

Suffrage should have appealed to the progressive minds who wrote the Oklahoma state constitution. But, two underlying factors can be seen as the reason women would have to fight for another eleven years before they won suffrage in Oklahoma. The first was the fear that woman suffrage would enfranchise black as well as white women; it concerned delegates who migrated to Oklahoma from the American South that woman suffrage may move the country closer to racial equality. The other reason for the failure was that anti-suffrage advocates feared women would align themselves with the Socialists, who enjoyed a significant third-party status in the early twentieth century. This threatened the Oklahoma Democrat party.[8]

From 1910 until 1917, there was little enthusiasm generated among Oklahoma women for the suffrage cause. Just prior to America's entrance into the first World War, the national suffrage association began to organize in the states. National leaders who came to Oklahoma instilled a new spirit into the campaign that seemed to be missing in previous attempts

2

The Age of Iron: Man as he expects to be. Currier and Ives, 1869. (Library of Congress)

to win suffrage. With full steam ahead, suffragists presented a suffrage bill to the state legislature in 1917. Even though there was less of an argument by state legislators over the idea of woman suffrage, the bill did not pass because of a clause that required a literacy test for voting. (The Supreme Court declared Oklahoma's grandfather clause unconstitutional. Requiring a literacy qualification was yet another way to discriminate against black voters, black women in particular.)

America's entry into World War I temporarily delayed suffrage activity in the state, but women's work for the war effort by serving on defense committees, selling war bonds, working for the Red Cross, or simply sewing uniforms gained them new respect and ultimately swung public opinion in favor of the amendment. The National Suffrage Organization also helped the Oklahoma crusade by funding suffrage activities throughout the state. Another factor in the success of the 1917 suffrage campaign was that suffragists had the endorsement of not only the Socialist party, but of the Republican and Democrat parties as well. On November 5, 1918, Oklahoma voters once again lined up at polling booths to cast their votes on the suffrage issue. Governor Robert L. Williams declared that woman suffrage had passed after waiting days for each county to tabulate their ballots and after a considerable challenge by the anti-suffrage forces.[9]

Until recently, little had been written about women's political activities after suffrage because low voter turnout among newly enfranchised women in the 1920s seemed to indicate that women were not interested in politics. However, Oklahoma women were quite active politically before and after woman suffrage. In part, their political activism can be explained by looking at the unique manner in which Oklahoma was settled in the late nineteenth century. The area that encompassed present-day Oklahoma was designated in the early nineteenth century by the United States government as Indian Territory. In March 1889, President Benjamin Harrison issued a proclamation declaring that certain areas of Indian Territory would be opened for settlement at noon on April 22, 1889. The publicity accompanying the preparations for opening generated such enthusiasm that it became apparent to government officials that there were more homesteaders than claims available. Consequently, planners decided that the most equitable way to issue the land was by a "run." People from all regions of the country and all walks of life—farmers, physicians, lawyers, ministers, teachers, merchants, along with single men and women, black and white—lined up at the starting line to begin

The Awakening, Hy Mayer, 1915. Torch-bearing female symbolizes the awakening of women to the desire for suffrage. She strides across the western states where women already have the vote toward the East where they reach out to her.

the race for the most desirable land. From this novel beginning, men and women immediately worked to transform the barren plains into farms, towns and communities, where they eventually built a market economy and political and social institutions that rivaled those of the communities they left behind.[10] Women played an important role in helping to change the raw frontier environment of 1889 into modernizing communities. One way in which they did this was by establishing women's organizations that offered them not only a social outlet, but also a forum to discuss the needs of their communities. Numerous women's clubs, with such intriguing names as Philomathea Study Club, Chautauqua Literary and Scientific Club, Coterie, Ladies of the Leaf, The Probiren, The Matron's Magazine, The Athenaeum, The Merrie Wives, and The Current Events, flourished throughout the Twin Territories. In their clubs, women joined together to promote self-improvement and education through the study of American history, poetry, art, and music. In 1898 many of the clubs in both Indian and Oklahoma Territories joined together to form the Oklahoma and Indian Territory Federation of Women's Clubs. The focus changed once the clubs organized into the national federation. The mission of the national organization moved away from "self culture" and stated the importance of studying issues concerning the welfare of society.[11] Much of the political activity of Oklahoma women before suffrage was through the Oklahoma Federation of Women's Clubs and the Women's Christian Temperance Union, where women fought to reform many aspects of American society.

Reform activity was an acceptable way for women in the nineteenth century to extend their influence from the home into the whole of society. By so doing, women established their presence in the public sphere where they acquired political skills and assumed leadership positions. Women justified this move into what was traditionally men's domain by believing that women's special qualities could help solve some of the nation's problems—especially problems resulting from the transformation of the country from a rural to an industrial economy. Many women believed that the new industrial culture was a threat to traditional American work and social values.[12] As more women became aware of the unhealthful deplorable conditions under which men, women, and children worked in industry, the more active women became in reform. Consequently, through their reform activities in the public sphere, women developed a philosophy that was outside the mainstream political thought of nineteenth and early twentieth-century America. Women offered a new definition concerning

6

the role of the state in governing American life; they introduced into the political arena the ideals of a welfare state, which promoted legislation to protect the lives and well-being of women and children.[13]

The work of Oklahoma women to secure legislation for the betterment of society continued after suffrage through new organizations such as the Women's Legislative Council, the League of Women Voters, and the National Woman's party. Women also had a different attitude about their role in politics. They took their responsibility as voting citizens quite seriously and believed that women should worked toward good government, which meant cleaning up the corrupt male bastion of state and local politics. How seriously did the male citizenry of Oklahoma take women's participation in politics? One way in which to answer this is to look at the attention given to Oklahoma women who participated in Oklahoma's political culture.

In the spring of 1920, the prominent Oklahoma political newspaper, *Harlow's Weekly*, started a new column entitled "Oklahoma Women in Politics."[14] The astute editors timed the column to coincide with the passage of the Susan B. Anthony Woman Suffrage Amendment by the United States Congress and the meeting of the Republican and Democrat Conventions in the summer of 1920. The weekly column described the furious activities of women as they organized, recruited, assembled, and traveled to participate in conventions and campaign for candidates, including women, in Oklahoma. The column is an important source for understanding women's involvement in politics after suffrage and their philosophy on the nature of government and its role in American life.

Oklahoma women went to the polls in substantial numbers to vote in the November 1920 national election. After a poor showing in the primary election in August of that year, the number of women voting in the general election surprised political observers; so much so that they contributed Republican victories in both national and state elections to the woman vote. Statistics help to put into perspective Oklahoma women's political participation after suffrage. The total vote in the 1920 election in Oklahoma was 489,130.[15] What surprised political observers was that the total was 197,130 more votes than were cast in the national election of 1916. It was estimated by *Harlow's Weekly* that 150,000 women voted in the election, or thirty percent of all votes cast, which explains the increase in voter participation in the state from the 1916 election.[16] Considering the lack of interest in woman suffrage by many of the state's women, the showing at the polls can be seen as remarkable and attest to

7

their determination to take political equality seriously. But, voting for a particular candidate or party was not the end all of their political culture. Their main concern was to continue with the political programs that they had set into motion long before they received the franchise.

As active as Oklahoma women were after suffrage, their political fervor seemed to wane by 1923. In that year, the editors of *Harlow's Weekly* changed the content of the "Oklahoma Women in Politics" column to less of a report on women's political activities and more of an account of the day-to-day events of club women. The different emphasis reflected the change in the role of Oklahoma women in politics and in the focus of their political activities. The shift occurred for several reasons. First, political gains by Republicans, who were elected to state and national offices in 1920, moved the country in a conservative direction; there was not the same fervor for progressive reform as there was at the end of the nineteenth century and the early twentieth century. But probably more of a factor was that Oklahoma women were anxious about changes taking place in society that resulted from the boom and bust cycle of Oklahoma's economy in the 1920s. Women were alarmed that traditional values based on a homogeneous Protestant community of democratic citizens, who still believed in Victorian morality, were falling by the wayside as a more modern society emerged in Oklahoma. The belief system that once motivated the political activities of Oklahoma women during the initial fight for suffrage turned more conservative as they tried to protect the American family and community from "foreign" influences. The political activities of Oklahoma women, motivated by their philosophy that spanned the political spectrum after suffrage, are the subject of this book. *Across the Political Spectrum: Oklahoma Women in Politics in the Early Twentieth Century* begins on the left with the political activities of Oklahoma women in the Socialist party and ends on the far right with the activities of women in conservative organizations such as the Women of the Ku Klux Klan.

NOTES

1. Quoted in J. Stanley Lemons, *The Woman Citizen, Social Feminism in the 1920s*, (Urbana: University of Illinois Press, 1973), p. 85.

2. Abbie B. Hillerman, *History of the Woman's Christian Temperance Union of Indian Territory, Oklahoma Territory and the State of Oklahoma*, (Sapulpa: Jennings Printing and Stationery Co., 1925), p. 12.

3. Mari Jo Buhle, *Women and American Socialism, 1870–1920*, (Urbana: University of Illinois Press, 1983), p. 60; After Frances Willard left Indian Territory in 1888, other reform-minded women visited the region helping Indian Territory women organize the WCTU. The organization spread to Oklahoma Territory after President Benjamin Harrison opened the area for settlement in 1889. By April, 1890, the first organization started work on legislation to safeguard or "purify" the new Oklahoma society. After statehood in 1907, the WCTU in Indian Territory and Oklahoma Territory joined together in one Union, the Oklahoma Woman's Christian Temperance Union. Hillerman, *History of the Woman's Christian Temperance Union*, p. 63.

4. Although discordant to the ear, the word "woman" suffrage instead of "women's" suffrage is the acceptable use of the term. See Nancy F. Cott, *The Grounding of Modern Feminism*, (New Haven: Yale University Press, 1987), p.3.

5. Quoted in Ida Husted Harper, *History of Woman Suffrage, 1900–1920*, Vol. 6, (New York: Arno and the New York Times, 1969), p. 520.

6. Ibid., pp. 521–22.

7. Ibid.

8. Ibid.

9. Mattie Louise Ivie, "Woman Suffrage in Oklahoma 1890–1918," (master's thesis, Oklahoma State University, 1971), p. 64.

10. H. Wayne Morgan and Anne Hodges Morgan, *Oklahoma: A History*, (New York: W. W. Norton and Company, Inc., 1977), p. 49; With President Harrison's proclamation, the area referred to as Indian Territory, encompassing the land that is the present state of Oklahoma, was divided into Oklahoma and Indian Territory. Victor E. Harlow, *Harlow's Oklahoma History*, (Norman: Harlow's Publishing Company, 1967), p. 204.

11. Susan L. Allen, "Progressive Spirit: The Oklahoma and Indian Territory Federation of Women's Clubs," *Chronicles of Oklahoma* 66 (Spring 1988):4 The change of focus in the literary club was noted by Angelo C. Scott in 1939, who wrote of one club, "Like its prototype [Philomathea] the Twentieth Century Club started as a study club, but through the years it took on, as did the others, all sorts of philanthropies, welfare work, and civic activities." Angelo C. Scott, *The Story of Oklahoma City*, (Oklahoma City: Times-Journal Publishing Co., 1939) p. 167; Major General Charles F. Barrett, *Oklahoma After Fifty Years: The Sooner State and Its People 1889–1939*, (Oklahoma City: The Historical Record Association, 1941), p. 382.

12. Karen Blair labels the women extension of the home into the greater society as "domestic feminism." Karen J. Blair, *The Clubwoman as Feminist: True Womanhood Redefined, 1868-1914*, (New York: Holmes and Meier Publications, Ind., 1980), p. 117.

13. Molly Ladd-Taylor labels these women as maternalist. She explained that "Maternalists were wedded to an ideology rooted in nineteenth-century doctrine of separate spheres and to a presumption of women's economic and social dependence," whereas Feminism encompassed "female individuality, political participation, and economic independence. Molly Ladd-Taylor, "Toward Defining Maternalism in U.S. History," *Journal of Women's History* 5 (Fall 1993): 110–113. Maternalism is almost the twin sister of social feminism, see Naomi Black, *Social Feminism*, (Ithaca: Cornell University Press, 1989).

14. *Harlow's Weekly* was a widely read political newspaper in Oklahoma in the early twentieth century. The publisher, Victor Harlow, began the newspaper August 17, 1912. The weekly paper informed Oklahomans about their state's political life until 1940. See Victor M. Harlow, *A History of Harlow's Weekly*, (Oklahoma City: Harlow Publishing, 1954).

15. *Daily Oklahoman* 4 November 1920.

16. *Harlow's Weekly* 19 November 1920. For a comparison, the 1996 national election statistics for Oklahoma indicates that women cast 60 percent of the vote. Reported Voting and Registration, by Sex, and Age, For States, November 1996, U.S. Bureau of Census, 1998.

Organizing on the Left: Oklahoma Women and the Socialist Party

W innie Branstetter, assistant state secretary of the Oklahoma Socialist Party, walked into the state headquarters of the Oklahoma Suffrage Association in 1910 to offer assistance in promoting suffrage for Oklahoma women. Ida Porter-Boyer, national suffrage organizer from Pennsylvania assigned to Oklahoma, regarded Branstetter's visit with caution; she was uncertain whether an affiliation with the Socialist Party would do more harm than good in promoting woman suffrage. She later wrote, "at that time all of us were wary of the effect socialism might have on our advocacy."[1] Woman suffrage was an important issue with Branstetter because she viewed women's votes an essential tool in building the Socialist party into one of the major political parties in America.

The Socialists sent Winnie and Otto Branstetter to the Southwest to organize for the party. They planned to arrive in the Twin Territories on the eve of statehood so they could have the opportunity to influence the writing of the new state constitution. Otto was a professional organizer from Chicago who wasted little time in coordinating state and national affiliation and in improving party organization in the newly formed state. A year after statehood in 1908, Oklahoma had a higher percentage of Socialists than any other state. The party rewarded Otto Branstetter by appointing him secretary-treasurer, and Winnie assistant state secretary. The Branstetters were typical of the men and women in the early twentieth century who worked to build socialism into a major third party by 1912. The Southwest was an ideal recruiting ground for Socialists because of the political void left by defunct agrarian movements of the late nineteenth century, and because of adverse economic conditions that kept farmers on the bottom rung of the prosperity ladder.[2]

Men and women suffered equally when depressed farm prices and high transportation and consumer costs affected their ability to make a living from farming. To better their situation, many rural people joined agrarian movements that called for a more equitable economic system. Women became involved in agrarian politics as early as the 1860s through such organizations as the Patrons of Husbandry. In the Patrons, or the Grange, women worked side by side with men on an equal basis to better the economic condition of the American farm family. Grange members believed that rural economic problems stemmed from an immoral economic system that allowed some individuals to amass fortunes at the hands of those who barely held subsistence-level existence. Women were important in the fight against the perceived inequitable economic order because Grange members believed women held special qualities that enabled them to "guide human existence."[3] Because the Grange considered women essential to the welfare of the family, women shared political equality with male members of the organization. Through women's experience in the Grange, they strengthened the western women's movement and prepared women for a broader role in politics.[4]

By the 1880s women started to campaign for the People's party and the principles of populism. Populists' ideology was a philosophical mix of Jeffersonian democracy and Christianity. Important was the ideal that all people should share in an equitable economic system based on productive labor. Especially important was a small unobtrusive federal government whose authority only extended to correct corporate abuse, which they viewed as a result of capitalism. The Populist program called for a fiat money system where specie had no inherent value, but was only a medium of exchange. To ease the farmer's burden, Populists championed nationalization of the railroads, utilities and control of land monopolies.[5] As in most agrarian movements, Populist women enjoyed political equality and believed that universal suffrage was important if women were to uphold the nation's traditional values. In the Southwest the Socialist party took up the agrarian cause when the Populist party began to wane at the end of the nineteenth century. The Socialist party incorporated many Populist principles, which also helped them to recruit from the Populist ranks.[6] The economically concerned farm wife, who adhered to the ideological principles of populism, could easily move her philosophical ideals to the Socialist party. From the rural countryside to the growing urban areas, the Socialist party in Oklahoma provided women a training ground for political activism that served them well in their fight for political reform in the early twentieth century.

The organization of the Socialist party began when Otto and Winnie Branstetter arrived in Oklahoma Territory in 1906. The

SUFFRAGISTS' MARCH TO THE CAPITOL, APR. 7, 1913, - #3

Suffrage march on the Capitol. April 7, 1913.

Who's Rocking the Cradle?

Branstetters were followers of Victor Berger, who along with Eugene Debs and Morris Hillquit, founded the Socialist party of America in 1901. It was not difficult for Oklahoma Socialists to establish a successful party organization. As early as 1895, they had organized their first meeting at Medford, where they wrote a party platform that reflected the principles of the late-nineteenth-century Populist. Socialists added to their plan universal suffrage regardless of sex, color, and creed. After the founding of a national organization, the party sent organizers into the Southwest to establish Socialist chapters. Oklahoma became fertile ground for recruitment because of rural discontent and the need for agricultural reform. Socialists began to view agriculture in the same light as industrial capitalism. An agricultural operation required capital and ownership of land, and market forces determined profit. Farm laborers, like their industrial counterpart, benefited little from their work. When Socialists began their work in Oklahoma, the major political parties did not address the farmer's problems. This left an opening for Socialists to propose programs to solve farmers' problems.[7]

Women's involvement in the Socialist movement began shortly after the organization of the national party in 1901. Initially, men in the party barely acknowledged the women's presence or their concern for economic and political equality. If anything, men believed women tended to dominate party meetings and that gender-based issues were not relevant to the economic struggle inherent in socialism. Because of the somewhat hostile reception they received by the rank-and-file, some women broke from the party in 1901 to organize the Woman's National Socialist League, and later the Woman's National Socialist Union. The purpose of these organizations was to teach the principles of socialism to women and to provide a platform for them to express their individual concerns. Not all women, however, thought that separate organizations would benefit their cause. Staunch party members believed that separate female organizations would create a club-like atmosphere that only imitated numerous other women's clubs of the times. The fear was that working-class women would be apprehensive about joining the Socialist ranks if the organization appeared to be for "club women." By the time of the Socialist Convention in Chicago in 1904, women abandoned the ideals of separate organizations and became active members in the party. In the beginning years, their involvement in party affairs was negligible; only eight women delegates attended the Convention. Women believed that they had made progress when the party included woman suffrage in the platform. The issue, however, appeared like an afterthought at the bottom of a long list of concerns.[8]

Four years later, at the 1908 Socialist Convention in Chicago, men were more receptive of women's participation in the party and of addressing women's issues. Part of this change in attitude emanated from the recommendation of the 1907 Second International Socialist meeting in Stuttgart, Germany. Delegates at the meeting adopted a resolution that called for Socialists to become more active in promoting women's interests, especially suffrage. In response to recommendations, the Socialist party created a Committee on Women at their 1908 Chicago Convention. The duty of committee members, consisting of nine comrades (eight women and one man), was to study women's relationship to the party. Their report suggested that it was in the party's interest to increase and improve party propaganda and organizational work among women. Women made further progress when the party added the Women's National Committee (WNC) as a permanent department within the party structure. The party offered little financial support for the activities of the WNC except to provide a salary for a woman organizer, whose responsibility it was to work in the field coordinating regional and state recruitment. As a result of the WNC's organizing efforts, women's Socialist groups grew in cities and towns throughout the United States.[9] Some of the women's organizations were separate from the men's groups, but for the most part, women organized within the party local. The WNC recommended establishment of programs to educate Socialist women on the issues, the thought being that women would then branch out over the countryside recruiting women into the party.

An important source used to educate women in Socialist doctrine was the *Socialist Woman*, a newspaper for women established in Chicago in 1907 by Japanese Socialist Kiichi Kaneko. The newspaper was a propaganda tool designed to educate women in the merits of socialism and to solicit their help in party recruitment. It also served as an informational clearinghouse to apprise the readership of the activities of Socialist locals throughout the country.[10] The *Socialist Woman* was an effective tool for increasing the number of Oklahoma women who joined the party. It is difficult to calculate the exact number, but typically, if their husbands belonged to the party, women were also members. Between the years 1904 and 1908, when women began to organize and there was a concentrated effort to sell subscriptions to the *Socialist Woman*, the Socialist vote in the state grew from 4,443 to 21,752.[11] Mrs. Ethel Bradshaw of Shawnee, Oklahoma, summed up the relationship of Socialist newspapers to party membership when she informed the *Socialist Woman*, "Please find the enclosed for a year's subscription to the *Socialist Woman*. My husband takes *The Appeal*, *The Ripsaw*, and *Wilshire's*, and now if there is a publication for boys we will subscribe for our little son, and then we will be a Socialist family out and out."[12] Oklahoma women realized the importance of the paper in providing information and as a source of communication between Socialist women throughout the country. Matilda H. Hodges of Stillwater, Oklahoma, explained to the editors, "We have a field to work to get the Socialist principles before the women. First let us get acquainted, then make every member of our organized body a worker, starting propaganda to pay for papers, magazines, and leaflets, the latter to be given away to women who don't know what socialism means."[13] Mrs. Irene Yeoman of Lawton, Oklahoma, concurred, "The Women need to be aroused more than men ... they do things when they wake up. So long may the *Socialist Woman* live."[14] Some Oklahoma women were more eloquent than others in expressing the value of the paper to the recruitment of women into the party. Mrs. Kate Stiles stated, "I believe I am not only voicing my own feeling but the sentiment of every intelligent reader of your paper when I say that words are inadequate to tell how we love you; how we honor the noble position you have taken, standing so bravely in the light, seeking to send its penetrating, purifying rays along every crooked path and into every foul corner."[15] Winnie Branstetter could have won an award for selling the most subscriptions to the *Socialist Woman* in Oklahoma. In almost every issue there was mention of Branstetter sending in her subscription money and names of new subscribers. In January of 1907, Branstetter sent the paper money for "a bundle" of the current issue to distribute at the state convention. Editors of the paper wrote of Branstetter, "If every reader of the *Socialist Woman* works as hard as Comrade Branstetter, our woman's movement will be something wonderful within a few years."[16]

Winnie Branstetter worked very hard in Oklahoma to recruit women into the Socialist party. She realized the importance of the *Socialist Woman* as a means of teaching Oklahoma women what socialism could mean to them and their future prosperity. In articles that she wrote for the newspaper, Branstetter elaborated on the virtues of socialism and how the Socialist party could better women's lives. She maintained that her own working-class background helped her to understand the oppression of American workers. She was born Winnie Shirley in Missouri in 1879. After attending Kansas City schools, she worked as a department store clerk until her marriage to Otto Branstetter in 1899. The couple subsequently moved to Oklahoma, where they maintained a farm in Cleveland

County. Their two daughters, Gertrude and Theresa, remembered that it was in Oklahoma that their parents "became converts to Socialism." But all other evidence indicates that Otto Branstetter was active in the Socialist party before moving to the state.[17]

In 1904 the Branstetters relocated to Norman, Oklahoma, where Otto worked as a paperhanger. Four years after settling in the Sooner State, Winnie moved her two girls to a homestead in Roswell, New Mexico. The purpose of the New Mexico interlude was to organize the New Mexico area for the Socialist party. With few resources, Branstetter conducted Socialist meetings in schoolhouses and lodge halls. As her daughter Gertrude later recalled, "Mother conducted most of the meetings alone, talking, teaching, distributing literature, debating local politicians, discussing local problems, and bringing the socialist interpretation to territorial and national economics and politics." Branstetter eventually became the first to hold the office of state secretary of the Socialist party in New Mexico. Once the government approved her claim to 160 acres, she sold the farm and rejoined her husband in Oklahoma City.[18]

Branstetter viewed woman suffrage as essential if Socialist women were going to change the economic and social evils accompanying the capitalist system. She was unlike many Socialist women, who devoted their efforts to obtaining economic equality for working-class women. Branstetter put aside class differences and worked with middle-class suffragists to help women attain the franchise. She was a member of the Norman, Oklahoma, suffrage organization and served for three years as vice president of the Oklahoma Suffrage Association. In 1912 Branstetter attended the National Suffrage Convention in Philadelphia as an Oklahoma delegate.[19]

Branstetter voiced her opinions on suffrage in her articles in the *Socialist Woman*. She often chastised the party for not taking an active stand on suffrage and recommended that the party pay less attention to reforming the capitalists and more attention to reform within the party. Branstetter urged the national party to accept resolutions, similar to those adopted by the Socialists in Oklahoma, that pledged strong support for woman suffrage.[20] In her arguments for suffrage, Branstetter maintained that it was not an issue of gender, but rather a question of economics; if there was sex discrimination, it was caused by capitalism. Branstetter directed her remarks to wives of Oklahoma tenant farmers, who along with their families, suffered a decline in agricultural markets and unfair economic disadvantage under the landlord system.[21] Southwestern Socialists lectured women that capitalism caused their economic situation, which forced them into the fields picking cotton. With suffrage, women could vote for Socialist candidates who advanced a more equitable economic system.[22]

Woman suffrage also would save the nation's youth from undue toil and labor. Branstetter pointed out that in Oklahoma child labor was just as much an issue as it was in industrial cities. Oklahoma's economy depended on raising cotton. Branstetter estimated that tenant farmers raised 75 percent of the state's cotton. The economic conditions were such that in order for a tenant family to make a living from cotton, every member of the family had to work in the fields. She wrote that, "We have a condition in Oklahoma bordering on feudalism, where the entire family, father, mother, and children, are forced to work in the fields in order to produce the barest necessities of life." Even the compulsory education law did not protect children from the rigors of fieldwork. Branstetter explained that the law only required children to attend school three months of the year, which left nine months for field labor. To Winnie Branstetter, the child labor problem would be solved by increasing the membership of women in the party and, therefore, increasing the voting strength of the working class.[23]

In February 1908 the Oklahoma Socialist party elected Branstetter assistant state secretary of the Oklahoma Socialists and appointed her as a delegate to the Socialist National Convention in Chicago.[24] While in Chicago, she attended the Women's Socialist League, a meeting to unite Socialist women and to address the question of suffrage. The delegates agreed that suffrage was an important tool with which to fight for their rights in an industrial world. They reasoned that women and men were physically and mentally equal and suffered under the same industrial conditions. Now that the working-class struggle included women, they, like their male counterparts, should be able to use their vote to better their condition. Women called on the party to take an active stand on the suffrage issue. They also believed that they must organize to fight for suffrage. As Branstetter told women, "I don't blame the men for overlooking us; they have enough to look after in fighting their own battles. We must fight for ourselves."[25]

While Winnie Branstetter fought for woman suffrage, other women leaders in the party directed their energies toward convincing women that capitalism would destroy the nuclear family. Socialist women were especially concerned with the effect that capitalism had on marriage and the home. Most agreed that women's place was in the home, where they contributed to the welfare of the family and society. The high divorce rate in the twentieth century indicated a breakdown in the family, which Socialist women viewed as a by-product of industrialization. Socialists argued that the capitalist system forced women into marriage for economic salvation, and that most women did not marry for love but out of "fear of hunger and starvation." If women were economically independent, they would not find it a necessity to marry but would do so for natural reasons such as love and companionship. Therefore, educating women to societal ills created by capitalism and the solutions provided by socialism would better the economic and social condition of women.[26]

One of the most outspoken advocates condemning capitalism for destroying the lives of women and children, and ultimately the home, was Kate Richards O'Hare. Like Branstetter, O'Hare fought for the Socialist cause in Oklahoma. Her oratorical skills and ability to reach her audience made her a popular speaker and one of the leading Socialists of the early twentieth century. Kate Richards was born March 26, 1876, on a 160-acre farm in Ottawa County, Kansas. Her family lost their farm in the drought of 1887 and subsequently moved to Kansas City, Missouri. There the family lived in relative poverty until her father secured permanent employment. It was during this period that Kate experienced the city environment of poverty, crime, and adverse industrial conditions. To help improve city conditions, O'Hare joined the Christian Endeavor Society, the Women's Christian Temperance Union, and the Florence Crittenton Missionary Society. She also attended Pawnee City Academy in Pawnee City, Nebraska, where she received her teaching certificate in 1894. She taught school for a couple of years but eventually resigned because of stress from overwork. O'Hare returned to Kansas City, where she moved in with her parents and secured a job as a secretary in her father's machinist shop. She acquired a share of the enterprise and entered the machinist crafts industry with a membership in the International Association of Machinists. Through her union activities, O'Hare became acquainted with the doctrines of socialism. She listened to Socialist speakers like "Mother" Jones and Julius A. Wayland, editor of the Socialist paper *Appeal to Reason*. In 1901 Kate moved to Girard, Kansas, to attend the International School of Social Economy, where she met Frank P. O'Hare. The two were married in Julius Wayland's home in Girard, Kansas, in 1902. Their honeymoon was a tour of the Midwest, where they lectured on socialism.[27] In 1904 the O'Hares moved to Chandler, Oklahoma Territory, where Frank accepted a job writing for the socialist-oriented newspaper the *Chandler Publicist*.[28] Kate began to organize Oklahoma women into the party shortly after moving to Chandler. She understood that an important tool in her campaign was distributing copies of the *Socialist Woman*. She wrote to the newspaper editors that she was impressed with the "chance" copies she was able to acquire in Chandler and wrote that, "I may be able to do some work for you here, and feel sure that I can send many subs. when I get out on the road again. The numbers I have seen are splendid, and I am sure the paper will fill a place in our propaganda that has long been void."[29]

Kate O'Hare was instrumental in building a strong grassroots Socialist organization in Oklahoma. She traveled throughout the state and the Southwest delivering the Socialist message in town meetings or at Socialist encampments.[30] The encampment, a camp meeting type forum borrowed from the Populists, was like a religious revival. Although the initial encampment was held outside Saline, Texas, in 1904, Frank O'Hare saw the effectiveness of such gatherings and recommended that Oklahoma Socialists schedule encampments across the state.[31] A typical summer season of encampments lasted more than four weeks. As one source noted, there were "sixty red-hot propaganda meetings a month, with an attendance of from 500 to 10,000 at each lecture." Under big canvas tents that could accommodate more than 1,000 people, Socialist speakers such as Eugene V. Debs, Oscar Ameringer, and Kate Richards O'Hare lectured Oklahoma farmers on how socialism could solve the high rate of farm tenancy by initiating cooperative land ownership.[32]

Kate O'Hare differed from Winnie Branstetter in the priority of her message to women. Branstetter fought to increase Socialist membership by explaining to women how suffrage was an important tool to be used to vote for candidates and programs that promoted the Socialist cause and, therefore, women's causes. Kate O'Hare crafted her message as more of an indictment against capitalism. O'Hare did agree with Branstetter that suffrage was a very important issue for women. Like Branstetter, O'Hare attended the Socialist Convention in Chicago in 1908 and joined Branstetter at the Women's Socialist League meeting. She informed the ladies at the meeting that the Republican party of Oklahoma planned to insert a plank in its platform supporting woman suffrage. The threat, she warned, was that Republicans would recruit the support of Oklahoma women. O'Hare urged Socialists to defeat the Republicans by actively supporting woman suffrage.[33]

Woman suffrage, however, was only one of many issues that concerned O'Hare. Like many Socialist women, O'Hare did not view suffrage as the solution to societal ills.[34] She believed that regardless of whether women could vote, the bigger issue was informing men and women of the possibilities of a socialist utopia, where all enjoyed the egalitarian world of a cooperative commonwealth. O'Hare pulled at the heart strings of her listeners with stories about the lives of women and children who toiled in factories or farm fields. She wrote about silk mill operators who hired young girls because "little girls have nimble fingers, and besides they are cheaper." And of the women, who had "stooped shoulders and dead faces."[35] O'Hare claimed that the factory environment would destroy for women "the joy of wifehood." The low wages that they earned and the high cost of living decreased women's chances for lasting love and marriage. O'Hare asserted that under socialism, children would know the joys of childhood, women the joys of wifehood, and all would enjoy the wealth of the universe.[36]

O'Hare also blamed the industrialist and his employment of children as one of the chief crimes of a capitalist society. Speaking from a street corner in front of the courthouse in Chandler, O'Hare lectured about the condition of children in factories and the evolution of the Trusts, showing the connection between private ownership of natural resources and the means of production. To O'Hare, the growth of industry and the wealth of Industrialists corresponded with the greater poverty of the workers, ultimately resulting in the necessity of children laborers.[37]

Winnie Branstetter and Kate Richards O'Hare were pioneers in speaking out on women's behalf during the early years of party organization. They were, however, part of a small minority of women who participated in party affairs. In 1908 women accounted for 10 percent of the delegates to the national convention. In all, only one-tenth of the membership in the Socialist party were women. But compared to the other major political parties, where less than 1 percent of the women participated in party politics, the Socialists had a significant female representation. After the establishment of the Women's National Committee, Socialist women were more visible and organized in their recruitment efforts. They appointed a general correspondent for the Women's National Committee and an Office of Woman's State Correspondent to act as a liaison for local, state, and national committees.[38]

Besides organizing communication networks between state and national committees, women participated in national speaking tours to recruit men and women into the Socialist party. Oklahoma and the Southwest was a popular region on the lyceum circuit. Kate Richards O'Hare was already well known throughout the country and especially Oklahoma. Next to O'Hare, Caroline Lowe was probably the most popular speaker in the Southwest. She was sent by the party to organize for Kansas and Oklahoma, where she presented her view of socialism to the farmers of the region. Lowe was born November 28, 1874 in Essex County, Ontario. By 1890 her family had relocated to Kansas City, Missouri. After graduating from Kansas City High School, Lowe obtained her teaching credential and taught school in the Kansas City system, where she also organized the first teachers' union in 1898. It was through her union activities that Lowe became acquainted with the tenets of socialism. By 1908 she abandoned the teaching profession and became a lecturer for the Socialist party. Lowe was also a member of the Women's National Committee and was the first to hold office as general correspondent.[39] As national lecturer and organizer for the party, Lowe first concentrated her recruitment work in the coal region of southeastern Kansas, organizing schoolhouse meetings to recruit women into the party. Lowe was also a popular speaker at Socialist encampments in Oklahoma. Throughout the summer encampment seasons, Lowe presented her views to Oklahoma farmers on the religious, political and economic conditions of the country.[40]

Lowe viewed women's struggle for political and economic equality from a historical perspective. In her testimony before congressional hearings on woman suffrage, Lowe explained that women once worked at home spinning, making bread, or making butter for a limited market. Women's status changed when machines and factory work replaced home industry. This change forced women into a workplace where they labored long hours for low pay under autocratic bosses. She agreed that suffrage would give women the self-protection they needed in the industrial workplace—a voice in making laws that affected their lives.[41] Women in Oklahoma echoed Lowe's analysis. Stella Ruch, from the Union Social Club, explained that woman suffrage was "an important question to every wage earning woman since the ballot is the only means whereby we could secure the laws which control our wages, hours of labor, and the many conditions which we are employed.... As voting workers we would cease to be cheap labor in the wage market."[42] Ruth Williamson of Shattuck, Oklahoma, wrote in the *Ellis County Socialist* that women should join the Socialist party because it was the only party to endorse woman suffrage, and that with suffrage, "Many evils now prevalent in the world, such as the whiskey traffic, will be eradicated when women have the privilege of asserting her rights at the ballot."[43]

While lecturing in Oklahoma and the Southwest, Lowe helped organize women in Kansas and Oklahoma into committees in their Socialist locals. One of Lowe's responsibilities as general correspondent for the WNC was to establish the monthly program for women to follow in their local meetings. Lowe informed committee chairmen that each meeting should begin with remarks from the chairman that introduced a specific subject, which Lowe provided. The subject for the March 1911 meeting was entitled "Socialism and the Home." According to the plan, the chairman would offer her introductory remarks, "You have heard that socialism will break up the home. We have gathered here this evening to discuss this subject, earnestly and quietly." A group sing would follow and then more lecture, "Only socialism has the cure for the great wrong of a homeless nation. Capitalism robs us of our homes, socialism makes possible a home for all." Again, a song, appropriately entitled "Our Happy Home," followed. As Lowe's program progressed, she crafted the indictment of the evils of capitalism to evoke an emotional response from the women gathered. In a story entitled "A Pension for Mothers," Lowe wrote for the chairman, "She was just a pale little woman, dressed in cheap mourning. She carried a pale little baby and two pale little children clung to her skirts." Programs throughout the summer and fall of 1911 discussed such diverse topics as "Social Diseases," and "Labor Legislation Affecting Women and Children."[44] The general correspondent did not send the program to individual locals, but circulated it through the *Socialist Woman*.

The brand of Socialism that interested Oklahoma women was infused with the evangelism that many Oklahomans embraced in the early twentieth century. Christian socialism appealed to Oklahoma women because they found the Biblical message compatible with the Socialist message.[45] It was, after all, the downtrodden and the poor with whom Jesus worked. And, the ideal that all are equal under the eye of God was more easily associated with socialism than capitalism. Mrs. Dora Mertz of Oklahoma City believed that the Bible condemned capitalism and lectured that God demanded that women "participate freely in the affairs of home, church, and state."[46] Women who were Christian pacifists also believed socialism would move all people toward world peace. Mrs. A. C. Hoefer of Driftwood, Oklahoma, wrote, "If we ever fulfill the will of our Savior we must consider our neighboring nations as our brothers and sisters in one great Christian Union.... We as mothers of the race should stand with helmet and shield at the head of the procession, marching and educating toward the grand union for a world of peace."[47] Women regarded socialism as God's salvation for women and mankind. As one lady remarked, "as we enter more and more into socialism, we mark a Sabbath day's journey toward God, brotherhood, and purity."[48]

When the Oklahoma party began to wane in 1916, so too did the work of Socialist women and their recruitment efforts in Oklahoma. The

23

Large group, mostly women, raising "No More War" banner over headquarters of National Council for Reduction of Armaments. The building is also the headquarters for National League of Women Voters on 17th Street, Washington, D.C. (1922).

Oklahoma Socialist party made significant gains in recruitment from 1907 until 1916. Eugene V. Debs, Socialist candidate for president, received 8 percent of the Oklahoma vote in 1908 and 16 percent in 1912. By 1914 the Socialist candidate for governor received 21 percent of the vote and five Socialists won state legislative offices. The gain in the ranks of Oklahoma Socialists held steady in 1916 but lost significant ground by 1918. The decline in the Socialist party after 1916 was due to President Woodrow Wilson's preparedness program and the eventual involvement of American forces in World War I.[49] At the Socialist Convention in St. Louis in 1916, the party took a stand against American involvement in the European conflict. This branded the party as pro-German and drew criticism from many sectors of American society. Even though the Oklahoma party did not endorse the antiwar stand, Socialists in the state spoke out against American foreign policy. This "un-American" attitude, along with radical activities of the Working Class Union, a militant tenant farmers union, that initiated draft riots called the Green Corn Rebellion throughout several Oklahoma counties, caused many to abandon the Socialist party in Oklahoma. Also significant was the improved economic condition of the farmers. President Wilson's economic programs to prepare America for involvement in the war temporarily enhanced the economic well-being of the country. In Oklahoma the federal government encouraged farmers to expand their acreage and encouraged the production of wheat and corn. Farmers often went into debt to do so, but the high price of commodities and the increased European demand assured economic success. The farming community no longer found socialism an attractive alternative to a good market economy. In 1917 Patrick S. Nagle, Socialist lawyer from Kingfisher, sponsored a resolution that disbanded the Socialist party in Oklahoma.[50]

There were other politically active Oklahoma women who chose a different route than socialism to solve the economic inequity and suffering of the less fortunate in Oklahoma society. One such individual was Kate Barnard. At the same time that Socialist women were trying to increase membership by recruiting women into the party, Kate Barnard, who held the same convictions as many Socialists, rose to significant political power in the state by her involvement in territorial and state politics. Like many reform- minded progressive women at the turn of the century, Kate Barnard had great compassion for those at the lower end of the socioeconomic scale. She quickly saw that the most effective way to work toward a more equitable society was through the political system. She was undaunted by the fact that, as a women, she had very little political power, and she did not approach reform by first fighting for her own political equality. Instead she influenced male politicians and worked her way into a political position in the new state of Oklahoma, where she fought to change the condition of many in the state who she believed suffered from an unfair advantage. Barnard's first foray into politics came when she won an appointment to represent Oklahoma at the St. Louis World's Fair in 1904. While in St. Louis, she attended numerous seminars, especially those emphasizing "sociological and humanitarian work." Between conferences, Barnard toured poverty-stricken areas of St. Louis and later wrote several articles for St. Louis newspapers on poverty, crime, and disease. When Barnard returned to Oklahoma, she studied to be a stenographer and took a job with the United Provident Association as its first matron. Her home became the distributing point for groceries, clothes, and medicine for the needy.

Barnard's interest in the conditions that caused poverty led her on a fact finding tour of the slums, factories, and workshops in industrial sectors of Eastern cities. After meeting with members of the National Child Labor Committee and other leading "sociologists" in the East, Barnard returned to Oklahoma to help fashion the state's first constitution into a progressive document that incorporated the welfare of needy Oklahomans. Barnard had three demands that she insisted politicians include in the state's constitution: child labor laws, compulsory education laws, and a Department of Charities in state government. To garner support for her program, she attended the state convention of farmers and laborers in Shawnee. But her most effective move was to confer with the chairman of the Democratic Campaign Committee. Ultimately, the Democrat party included Barnard's three proposals in the party platform. In return, Barnard campaigned for the party and helped to elect a majority of Democrats to the constitutional convention. Barnard was an effective orator and was politically respected in the Democrat party. She became the first candidate for Commissioner of Charities and Corrections. Her election victory was impressive in that she carried a majority of the vote in the state's Republican strongholds.[51]

Barnard's self-motivated style and penchant to accomplish what many would consider impossible goals, made her an effective spokeswoman for the woman suffrage cause. Barnard's objective, however, was to be successful in her own work, which she considered paramount to the fight for woman suffrage. In letters to those who asked for her help in the suffrage battle, she frequently offered the same excuse, "My life has been too busy and my mind filled with too many other things to give much attention to the question of woman's suffrage."[52] Historians have misunderstood Barnard's lack of interest in woman suffrage and tend to assign her position on the issue to the antisuffrage camp. Barnard was not opposed to suffrage, just indifferent. When questioned, she would point out that, while living in Denver, she was a voting citizen. But she was also quick to explain that she came away from the experience realizing that women's vote was just as easily bought as that of men. "I was not particularly edified by it because I saw that women were herded just like men, and made to vote as the interest saw fit."[53] Barnard saw no reason why she should support woman suffrage when she had accomplished so much without it. She criticized the suffragists for their high-handed tactics and lack of political savvy and chastised them for their failure to gain support for woman suffrage at the constitutional convention and the meeting of the first two legislatures, even though women had lobbied quite extensively for their cause. Barnard on the other hand boasted that she "went in single-handed and secured three propositions in the constitution and twenty-two laws in two legislatures."[54] Part of Barnard's stand on suffrage emanated from her unfavorable impression of the suffragists, many of whom did not help Kate in her charitable work. She reported that, "I have never received one particle of assistance from women in my campaign for bettering the conditions of the wage-earner, the children, and the poor and needy." She believed that the reason men were more giving of their time and assistance was that they were not as envious of Barnard's success as were most women. "In my charity work, I have felt the full force of their jealousies and unreliability." Barnard also found it disconcerting that suffragists threatened to blacklist her, working to defeat her at the polls if she did not lend her name and energies to the suffrage cause. She concluded that, "I cannot work in concert with a flock of old hens who would do me this way."[55]

As Commissioner of Charities and Corrections, Kate Barnard did use her energies to fight to better the conditions of men, women, and children who were wards of the state. In 1908 she fought for more humane treatment of Oklahoma prisoners housed at the Lansing, Kansas, penitentiary. From her investigation of the conditions in which prisoners lived, the state of Oklahoma broke its contract with Kansas for the care of more than 600 Oklahoma prisoners. Barnard's investigation of Indian orphans resulted in the funding of two million dollars to investigate and prosecute graft and corruption by those who became the guardians of Indian children. Especially troublesome was the apparent practice of guardians selling off orphans' land, which was to the economic advantage of the guardians. Barnard's investigation of the land grab met with a cool reception by lawmakers. Her continual fight for her department's appropriations to further her investigation damaged her in two ways; Barnard's health started to deteriorate, and funding to her department was cut to the point that she could no longer wage her fight against corruption in state agencies.[56] Ultimately, Kate Barnard and her causes, like that of the Socialists, became irrelevant as Oklahoma's political and economic life matured, and pioneer citizens resolved the conflicts inherent in frontier settlement.

Winnie Branstetter, Kate Richards O'Hare, Caroline Lowe, and Kate Barnard stand out as prominent Oklahoma women in politics in the presuffrage era of the early twentieth century. Their political activism evolved from their perception that an inequitable economic system created hardships and poverty for many Oklahomans. Although each one of these ladies left a legacy for future political activism by Oklahoma women, their involvement in state affairs was brief. Political misfortunes caused Otto and Winnie Branstetter to leave Oklahoma in 1913. Fighting within the Oklahoma Socialist party forced Otto Branstetter out. Many considered him an outsider from Chicago and refused him a seat at the state convention. The Branstetters moved to Chicago, where Otto eventually became executive secretary of the National Socialist party and Winnie continued her involvement in the Women's National Committee, succeeding Caroline Lowe as general correspondent. During the war years, Winnie Branstetter served as liaison from the national office to antiwar Socialist activists imprisoned at Leavenworth, Kansas. In 1921 she represented Cook County, Illinois, as a delegate to the Amnesty International Conference held in Washington, D.C.[57]

Frank and Kate Richards O'Hare moved from Chandler, Oklahoma, to Kansas City, Kansas, in 1909. Kate continued her work for the party and was elected to the National Executive Committee in 1910. In that year, O'Hare also ran for Congress, the first women to do so from Kansas. A few months after her failed candidacy, both Frank and Kate accepted positions as editors of the Socialist newspaper, the *National Rip-Saw*. In 1917 O'Hare served as chairwoman of the *War and Militarism Committee* at the St. Louis Emergency Convention and was elected international secretary of the Socialist party.[58] With the approaching American involvement in the European conflict, Kate O'Hare became an outspoken critic of American foreign policy. Officials of the federal government arrested her for her anti-war stand, and she spent four years in Missouri

State Penitentiary. After her release, she put her energy into prison reform for women. She died in 1948.[59]

Unlike Branstetter and O'Hare, Caroline Lowe never took up residence in Oklahoma. She did, however, spend a significant amount of time in the state working the encampment circuit to recruit for the party. Similar to O'Hare, Lowe ran for political office, managing a 35 percent return in the 1914 election for the Kansas State Legislature. Also in 1914, she enrolled in law school and four years later the state of Kansas admitted her to the Bar. During the war years, Lowe defended members of the Industrial Workers of the World who were on trial in various Midwest cities for antiwar activities. In 1923 she served as the official counsel for the United Mine Workers. Lowe continued practicing law in Pittsburg, Kansas, until her death in 1933.

During Kate Barnard's tenure as the first Commissioner of Charities and Corrections, she found it difficult to accomplish all that she set out to achieve. From the very beginning of her term, she understood that she was not afforded the same "quality" perks as the male members of Governor Charles N. Haskell's administration. From the worn-out conveyance that escorted her to the swearing-in ceremony to the assignment of her "pigeonhole" office, Barnard felt the discrimination. Placing her on the Democrat party ticket was necessary because she was instrumental in constructing the state constitution. But, as she later wrote, "Many referred to me as the Spiritual Life of the Statehood Battle. I was grateful to the Party Leaders who placed me on the State Ticket. I loved and believed in them and I supposed they returned that Trust and that Affection .... I expected Happiness when I reached the State House ... but they hid me away."[60]

It is difficult to categorize Barnard into any particular political slot because she was not motivated by party politics or economic and social theory, but only from what she could personally accomplish in improving the condition of mankind. Women found her difficult to understand because she did not use her political influence to fight for woman suffrage or women's causes. Even though she aligned with state Democrats, her friends and comrades were Socialists, particularly Pat Nagle and labor boss Pete Hanraty. The occasional newspaper column she submitted attested to Barnard's sympathies with the Socialist cause to the *Appeal to Reason*.[61] Historians have a difficult task in assigning Barnard to the Socialist party. There is little concrete evidence to support such an assumption. Instead Barnard is tagged with vague phrases such as "social justice advocate," or "social justice progressive."[62] Either way, it is evident that Barnard was more ideologically Socialist than she was Democrat or Republican. It can be assumed, perhaps, that to accomplish her goals she found it expedient to align with the party most likely to establish Oklahoma's first state government. At any rate, she stands out in Oklahoma history as an influential woman who, like many Socialist women, paved the way for Oklahoma women to participate in politics in the twentieth century.

NOTES

1. Howard L. Meredith, "History of the Socialist Party in Oklahoma," (Ph.D. dissertation, University of Oklahoma, 1969), p. 70; Oscar Ameringer, *If you Don't Weaken*, (Norman: University of Oklahoma Press, 1983), p. 189; James R. Green, *Grass Roots Socialism: Radical Movement in the Southwest 1895–1943*, (Baton Rouge: Louisiana State University Press, 1978), p. 39.

2. Meredith, "History of the Socialist Party in Oklahoma," p. 70.

3. Mari Jo Buhle, *Women and American Socialism 1870–1920*, (Urbana: University of Illinois Press, 1983), pp. 82–84.

4. Ibid.

5. John Thompson, *Closing the Frontier: Radical Response in Oklahoma, 1889–1923*, (Norman: University of Oklahoma Press), pp. 87, 90.

6. Ibid, p. 232. For the similarities between the Populist and Southwest Socialist see James R. Green, *Grass-Roots Socialism Radical Movements in the Southwest 1895–1943*, (Baton Rouge: Louisiana State University Press, 1978), p. 23.

7. Meredith, "History of the Socialist Party in Oklahoma," p. 20; Green, *Grass Roots Socialism*, p. 12.

8. *Socialist Woman*, July 1907, November 1907, January 1909; Sally M. Miller, "Woman in the Party Bureaucracy: Subservient Functionaries," in Sally M. Miller, ed., *Flawed Liberation Socialism and Feminism*, (Westport: Greenwood Press, 1981), p. 13; Bruce Dancis, "Socialism and Women in the United States, 1900–1917," *Socialist Revolution* 27 (1976): 81–144.

9. Dancis, "Socialism and Women in the United States, 1900–1917," pp. 370–372; *Encyclopedia of the American Left*, (New York: Garland Publishing, 1990), p. 830.

10. Buhle, *Women and American Socialism*, 1870–1920, p. 148.

11. The figures were taken from the Socialist Party of America Papers, microfilm, reel 110.

12. *Socialist Woman*, April 1908.

13. *Socialist Woman*, June 1907.

14. *Socialist Woman*, August 1907.

15. *Socialist Woman*, October 1910.

16. *Socialist Woman*, January 1907, October 1907.

17. *Oklahoma Pioneer*, 29 October 1910; Gertrude Branstetter Stone and Theresa Branstetter Taft, "Homesteading in New Mexico 1908–1909," Manuscript, Department of Special Collections, McFarland Library, University of Tulsa, Tulsa, Oklahoma.

18. Ibid.

19. John William Leonard, *Who's Who in America*, (New York: American Commonwealth Company, 1914), p. 123.

20. *Socialist Woman*, February 1908.

21. *Oklahoma Pioneer*, 9 March 1910.

22. *Oklahoma Pioneer*, 16 February 1910.

23. *Progressive Woman*, July 1912.

24. *Socialist Woman*, June 1908.

25. *Socialist Woman*, June 1908.

26. Miller, "Woman in the Party Bureaucracy: Subservient Functionaries," in Sally M. Miller, ed., *Flawed Liberation: Socialism and Feminism*, (Westport: Greenwood Press, 1981), pp. 13–35. Bruce, *Socialism and Women in the United States, 1900–1917*, p. 81.

27. *Socialist Woman*, October 1908; Neil Basen, "Kate Richards O'Hare: The First Lady of American Socialism," *Labor History* (November 1980): 168–199.

28. Sally M. Miller, *From Prairie to Prison: The Life of Socialist Activist Kate Richards O'Hare*, (Columbia: University of Missouri Press), p. 33.

29. *Socialist Woman*, May 1908.

30. Basen, "Kate Richards O'Hare," p. 174.

31. Green, *Grass Roots Socialism*, p. 40.

32. "The Oklahoma Encampment," *International Socialist Review* 10 (1909).

33. *Socialist Woman*, June 1908; Green, *Grass Roots Socialism*, p. 90.

34. Miller, "Women in the Party Bureaucracy," p. 27.

35. *Chandler Publicist*, 21 June 1904.

36. *Chandler Publicist*, 25 February 1905, 11 May 1905.

37. *Chandler Publicist*, 27 June 1905.

38. Miller, "Women in the Party Bureaucracy," pp. 16–17.

39. *Encyclopedia of the American Left*, p. 437.

40. *Vinita Daily Chieftain*, 12 September 1906.

41. U.S. Congress, Senate, Joint Committee of the Committee in Judiciary and the Committee on Woman Suffrage, Woman Suffrage, Hearings Before a Joint Committee on Woman Suffrage, March 13, 1912, 62d cong., 2d sess., 1912, pp. 16–20.

42. *Oklahoma Pioneer*, 13 October 1910.

43. *Ellis County Socialist*, 19 August 1915.

44. *Socialist Woman*, March 1911, July 1911, October 1911.

45. Meredith, "Oscar Ameringer and the Concept of Agrarian Socialism," *Chronicles of Oklahoma* XLV.

46. *Sword of Truth*, 26 March 1913; *Oklahoma Social Democrat*, 21 May 1913.

47. *Constructive Socialist*, 17 April 1912.

48. *Industrial Democrat*, 10 January 1910.

49. Garin Burbank, "The Disruption and Decline of the Oklahoma Socialist Party," *Journal of American Studies* 7 (August 1973): 133–152.

50. Meredith, "History of the Socialist Party in Oklahoma," p. 142.

51. Catherine Ann (Kate) Barnard was born in Geneva, Nebraska, in 1878. She moved to Oklahoma in 1889 after her father, John Barnard, staked a claim to land near Newalla. Kate lived on the Newalla farm while her father practiced law in Oklahoma City. She eventually moved to Oklahoma City, where she attended public school and St. Joseph's Academy. After finishing her education, Kate taught school for a while but left teaching to further her interest in bettering the condition of the less fortunate in society. "Excerpts from an Address by Mrs. Mabel Bassett before the Jeffersonian Club, March 3, 1941," *Voice of the Democratic Women of Oklahoma*, Anna Korn Collection, Oklahoma Historical Society, Oklahoma City, Oklahoma. See also Linda Reese, *Women of Oklahoma, 1890–1920*, (University of Oklahoma Press, 1997), chapter seven.

52. Kate Barnard to Miss Jean M. Gordon, 11 August 1908, Department of Charities and Corrections Collection, Archives, Oklahoma Department of Libraries, Oklahoma City, Oklahoma. Hereafter cited ODL.

53. Kate Barnard to Mrs. L. B. Snider, 19 June 1909, Department of Charities and Corrections Collections, ODL.

54. Ibid.

55. Kate Barnard to Miss Jean M. Gordon, 11 August 1908, ODL.

56. "Excerpts from an Address by Mrs. Mabel Bassett before the Jeffersonian Club, March 3, 1941," Anna Korn Collection, Oklahoma Historical Society, Oklahoma City, Oklahoma. See also, Angie Debo, *And Still the Waters Run*, (University of Oklahoma Press, 1984), p. 184.

57. Socialist Party of America Papers, Microfilm, roll 9.

58. Basen, "Kate Richards O'Hare," p. 168.

59. Mari Jo Buhle, Paul Buhle, Dan Georgakas, eds., *Encyclopedia of the American Left*, (New York: Garland Publishing, Inc. 1990)

60. Quoted in Reese, *Women of Oklahoma 1890–1920*, p. 203.

61. See *Appeal to Reason*, 11 March 1916.

62. Green, *Grass Roots Socialism*, 1895–1943, pp. 58, 63, 73.

WOMAN SUFFRAGE IN WYOMING TERRITORY.—SCENE AT THE POLLS IN CHEYENNE.
FROM A PHOTO. BY KIRKLAND.—SEE PAGE 200.

Woman suffrage in Wyoming. Scene at polls in Cheyenne. Frank Leslie's
Illustrated Newspaper, Nov. 24, 1888.

After Suffrage:
Political Parties and
the Woman Vote

Speaking before Oklahoma City Democrats in November 1919, Myrtle Archer McDougal, Democrat national committeewoman from Oklahoma, outlined the need to educate newly enfranchised Oklahoma women to the fundamental principles that underscored Democrat party doctrine. The committeewoman believed that by so doing, the party would increase membership and, they hoped, political power in the state. McDougal explained that the existing political alignment of both the Republican and Democrat parties was made up of staunch supporters who were not going to switch party affiliations. There was, however, another untapped source ready for political recruitmen—the woman voter. "The first political party," McDougal concluded, "that fully realizes that women are actual citizens, and that they are subject to the influences of facts and of an appeal to their judgment, is going to seize and retain the reins of political power in Oklahoma."[1]

Capturing women's vote and support in the parties was important in the unsettled political climate of post–World War I America. High inflation, unemployment, farmers' rebellion, and social unrest marked the postwar period. Many blamed the ailing President, Woodrow Wilson, for not implementing the same efficient methods in demobilization of the war machinery as he did in his initial military buildup. Additionally, the Red Scare generated public fear that there would be a radical revolution in the country. By 1920 the American people saw disunity, chaos, and a failure of Democrats to solve America's problems. With public sentiment moving over to the Republican column, the badly splintered Republican party became more unified and presented to the American people a plan for postwar recovery that the Democrats could not match.[2] The possibility of a political upset in the presidential election of 1920 caused the membership of both parties to view the new woman voter in terms of party strength. However, while men saw the quantitative value of recruiting women into the party organization, women viewed party membership as an opportunity to contribute to the political process and a way to urge the parties to include women's issues in the platforms. Men and women also did not always share the same loyalty to party principles or agree on the issues or the solutions to societal problems. Men accepted women into the party organization out of necessity, and this made it difficult for women to participate equally in party matters. But women viewed involvement in party politics as a logical conclusion to the long struggle for women's political equality and assumed that they would be able to affect change in American society through the party system. They found that this was not always the case. But, there were other benefits. For many Oklahoma women, political parties provided an avenue to perfect their political skills and an opportunity to discuss with one another issues that were of concern to all women.[3]

The first opportunity for Oklahoma women to take an active role in party politics was in July 1920 at the National Republican Party Convention in Chicago. In the twenty-member delegation from the Sooner state, the Oklahoma Republican party included two women delegates, Lola Clark Pearson of Marshall and Mrs. Frank Northrup of Oklahoma City. The 1920 convention was the first time in Republican history that women attended as delegates, but not the first time women attended in some official capacity. In 1892 the party chose three women as alternates to the Republican Convention. And in 1918, when it was apparent that the woman suffrage amendment would be ratified by the states, Republican chairman William H. Hayes asked Ruth Hanna McCormick of Illinois to head a National Women's Executive Committee of the Republican National Committee (RNC). The following year, the RNC appointed four women to the Republican council.[4] In 1920, when the Republicans held their convention in Chicago, twenty-seven women delegates and 131 alternates took their seats on the convention floor.[5]

Being chosen as a party delegate was only half of the battle facing women who wanted political equality in the party organization. Republican party leaders at first were hesitant to accept women; they resisted women's participation in party councils and allowed them a very small voice in party matters.[6] This was especially true in the Oklahoma delegation, where the two women delegates found it difficult to gain the acceptance of party leaders. It was obvious to the women that the Oklahoma Republican party did not immediately embrace women into

THE DAILY OKLAHOMAN

OKLAHOMA CITY, FRIDAY, JUNE 4, 1920

All Is Ready For Gong At Chicago Convention

Chicago, June 3 (special)
"Gentlemen, be seated"
This is what Col. Edwin P. Thayer, republican national sergeant-at-arms, will say, figuratively, to the 20,000 0r 25,000 delegates and visitors to the republican national convention in Chicago, June 8. He may add "likewise ladies," because under the banners of the state delegations there will be many delegates wearing hats, unless the sergeant-at-arms compels the women delegates to remove their headgear.

In other words, everything is in readiness for the big quadrennia; republican show, which this year promises to be "bigger and better than ever."

Daily Oklahoman, June 4, 1920

the party structure, and they noted that the decision to include women in the delegation to the national convention was, evidently, a difficult one. A telegram to Lola Pearson informing her that the state committee chose her as a delegate from the Fifth District illustrates the point. "After a most vicious fight lasting more than three hours, the Republican Committee unanimously voted approval of your contest in Fifth District, so please be sure to arrive in time to be seated."[7] Even though Pearson and Northrup were experienced in public service, they had little expertise in playing the "game" of politics. Their lack of political savvy encumbered their ability to influence the political debate. But they were rookies, and it was a learning situation. The women became aware soon after arriving at the convention that they would have little, if any, political clout within the Oklahoma delegation. The male delegates ignored the women, not primarily because of gender, but because the women aligned themselves with the "wrong" political faction within the party. Party infighting started at the state convention over the selection of the party's national committeeman. The contest was between oilman Jake L. Harmon of Ardmore and James J. McGraw of Oklahoma City. Those who supported Harmon for committeeman also supported Harding for President. Those who aligned with McGraw supported the presidential candidacy of General Leonard Wood. At the convention, the Harmon-Harding people had more delegates support than the McGraw-Wood faction. The two women delegates, however, supported McGraw-Wood, which left them out of the power structure of the party. The Wood campaign arranged for the women to stay at the Stratford Hotel with other Wood delegates. It was all very attractive to the Oklahoma women. The Wood people arranged a "Ladies' Parlor" for the women delegates where an after-lunch speaker tried "to boost Wood enthusiasm."[8] By supporting the minority candidate, the women had no voice in the Oklahoma meetings in Chicago. The editor of *Harlow's Weekly* later explained, "Women will have to take the same chances the men do, and get in 'right' or take their defeat graciously."[9]

Male members of the national party organization understood that women needed to be given a role in party affairs. Women were, after all, a significant voting population. In Chicago, the party expanded women's participation by electing five women assistant secretaries and appointing women to various committees including the Committee on Permanent Organization and the Committee on Rules and Order of Business. Party leaders also assigned women the honor of placing in nomination those seeking office. Women of all regions of the country from Mrs. Corinne

HARLOW'S WEEKLY
A Journal of comment and current events for Oklahoma
Victor E. Harlow, Editor

September 10, 1920

Oklahoma Women in Politics
By Nelle Bunyan Jennings

The republican women in the state officially opened their intensive speaking campaign beginning Monday of the current week. A "flying squadron" composed of seven women of national prominence in club, social, and professional circles, visited every congressional district in the state and spoke at many different points daily during the entire week

Those who visited Oklahoma, sent by the national headquarters, are Mrs. Margaret Hill McCarter of Kansas, Miss Perele Lucille Dunham of Chicago, Mrs. Sarah Sherman Maxon of Chicago, Mrs. W. W. Remington of Minneapolis, Mrs. Frank Dodson of Iowa, Mrs. Wm. Sprague of Chicago, Mrs. Robert J. Burdette of Los Angeles and Miss jean Hyde of Salt Lake City, Utah.

The speakers arrived in Oklahoma City on Monday Morning and were honor guests in the afternoon at a large reception in the ballroom of the Huckins hotel. Mrs. Clarence L. Henley of Oklahoma City, advisory board member from the Fifth District, was chairman of the reception committee.

On Monday night the women held a rally downtown, roping off a section of Main street north of the Huckins hotel, and providing seats for the audience.

The ladies spoke from an improvised platform erected on a truck and gaily decorated with bunting. There was a big crowd out to hear the distinguished speakers and they were cordially received.

Beginning Tuesday, the squadron made 75 speeches at the different cities and towns they had been scheduled to visit. Elaborate preparations were made by the republicans to entertain the visitors throughout the state.

Roosevelt Robinson of New York (Theodore Roosevelt's sister) to Miss Delle Boyd of Nevada, climbed the convention podium to place in nomination their candidate for president. However, women wanted more than token representation on committees or highly visible positions on the convention floor. Their main concern was obtaining equal representation within the party at the national and state level. The women reasoned that if they shared equal voting privileges with men, then women should also share equally in the responsibilities of party governance and in the nomination process. If there was more equal representation at the state level, more women would be appointed as delegates to the national convention and, therefore, be included in the decision making process.[10] Women, then, fought to change the party rules concerning the gender makeup of the Executive Committee of the RNC. The ladies believed it only fair that the committee should have an equal number of men and women. Women delegates met with the Rules Committee to voice their demands. The committee did not agree on the rule change, but offered an alternative: expansion of the executive committee from ten to fifteen members, seven women and eight men.[11]

While women fought for equal authority in the party, they also sought to influence the party platform that defined the Republican party position on election issues. Foremost on the women's list was insertion of a woman suffrage plank in the platform. This was not a difficult task because the Republicans were already on record for their support of suffrage. At the 1916 Republican Convention, the five women delegates plus representatives from the National American Woman's Suffrage Association presented their case to the Resolutions Committee that the party must support woman suffrage. In 1919 the Republican Congress passed the Susan B. Anthony Suffrage Amendment and sent it to the states for ratification.[12] Because the Republican party took the political gamble and supported ratification of the suffrage amendment, many believed that it was now up to them to get out in front on the issue and convince state legislatures to ratify it. The National Women's Party, the militant wing of the suffrage fight, sent representatives to the convention hoping to convince the Republicans to endorse speedy ratification so that women would be able to vote in the November presidential election. It was an easy win for the suffragists, most of whom at the convention supported ratification as soon as possible.[13] The party passed a resolution urging Republicans in the Tennessee Legislature, the 36th state needed to pass the federal amendment, to "vote unanimously for ratification."[14]

After Suffrage: Political Parties and the Woman Vote

The Republican platform reflected many of the concerns of women in the 1920s, including the protection of women in the workforce. One of the demands of the women delegates was that the Republicans continue their support for government appropriations for the Women's Bureau in the federal government.[15] The creation of a Women's Bureau resulted from studies of working women conducted by the United States Department of Commerce and Labor between 1907 and 1909. The reports revealed that the condition of women working in industry was far worse than many had imagined. Women's groups such as the General Federation of Women's Clubs, the National Women's Trade Union League, the Young Women's Christian Association, and the National Consumers' League, called for a bureau in the federal government that would provide special counsel to represent and protect wage-earning women. But it was not until the industrial buildup for World War I that there was an acute need for an agency to oversee laws protecting women in industry. The immediate nature of the problem stemmed from increased industrial output during the war years that inspired some state legislatures to overturn or simply not enforce hard-fought laws that protected women workers. To remedy the problem, in 1918 the federal government created an Advisory Council to the Secretary of Labor, which recommended a special bureau to consider the concerns of working women. After the war women lobbied for a continuation of congressional appropriations to extend the life of the bureau. In 1919 the Republican Congress continued funding but cut the bureau's budget from $150,000 to $40,000.[16] To ensure that the federal government continued to provide protection for women workers, Republican women proposed a plank for the continuation and expansion of the bureau. The plank in the platform acknowledged that women had special employment problems that warranted study and, therefore, recommended the establishment of a permanent Women's Bureau in the Department of Labor to "serve as a source of information to the states and to Congress." Other planks in the platform that reflected women's influence were ones that addressed the issue of men and women receiving equal pay for equal work and one limiting the work hours of women in industry.[17] The Republicans also included a plank in their platform that endorsed full citizenship for married women. Many women were under the assumption that passage of the nineteenth amendment guaranteed them the same rights enjoyed by men under the United States Constitution. The passage of suffrage, however, would not change laws that disqualified women from sitting on juries or running for some state offices. Also, under a 1907 federal statute, women married to resident aliens lost their American citizenship and automatically became citizens of their spouses' countries, even though the couples continued to reside in the United States. As residents of other countries, these women could not inherit property or buy real estate in the United States. In some states, including New York, women married to foreigners could not teach school, could not obtain a state job, and could not hold any elected or appointed office in government. As America moved closer to its involvement in the European conflict in 1917, immigrants and their spouses experienced even more restrictions on their freedoms. Authorities classified women married to resident aliens, especially those from Eastern Europe, as enemy aliens. The government seized their property and placed them under surveillance.[18] At the outset of the Republican National Convention, women fought for a plank in the platform recommending an overturn of the 1907 statute and a return of full citizenship to women.[19]

Men and women in the Republican party supported protective legislation, especially for women in the workforce, but not legislation that expanded the federal government's authority to the point where it might interfere with individual liberty. The Republicans typically did not support legislation that expanded the federal government to assume a more paternalistic role in American life. But one of the issues confronting them in the 1920 political campaign was congressional passage of the nation's first welfare legislation, the Sheppard-Towner Maternity and Infancy Bill. The bill provided a matching fund appropriation of $4,000,000 to the states for maternity and infant care.[20] Republican women at the Chicago Convention did not support the welfare legislation. Instead, they supported a plank in the platform that only called for better coordination between federal, state, and local health agencies. The Republicans were also tepid on supporting the establishment of a Department of Education in the federal government. This was an issue that divided politically active women. The need for the federal government to oversee the education of the country's youth became apparent to women when they learned that many of the young men drafted to serve their country in the first World War were illiterate. Republican presidential candidate Warren G. Harding addressed the concern when he announced that, if elected, he would establish a Department of Social Welfare in his administration, which would include an Assistant Secretary of Education. His program had more opponents than supporters; after Harding won the presidency, he shelved the plan.[21] At their convention, Republicans suggested that federal money allocated for education "be so directed as to awaken in the youth the spirit of America and a sense of patriotic duty to the United States."[22]

In most respects, women were successful in Chicago in establishing themselves as active party members and in coming together to discuss the problems in American society that were of concern to all women. Before suffrage, women were accustomed to working behind the scenes quietly and, sometimes not so quietly, urging men to implement legislative programs that would benefit women, children, and the family. With political equality, women came to center stage and believed that they could work, as men had always done, through the political system to initiate programs to better society. But, as Oklahoma's women delegates discovered, it was not that easy to assume a significant role or voice in party affairs. And the fact that the two women delegates were not appointed to any committees and were not asked to nominate a candidate to office attested to the lack of mentorship and support for the women by Republican men from Oklahoma.

Regardless, when Republican women returned to the Sooner State after the convention, they set out to recruit women into the party by explaining the concerns the Republicans had for the general welfare of women. It was not a difficult task to prove that Republicans held women's best interest at heart. It was, after all, the Republican Congress who passed the Susan B. Anthony Suffrage Amendment to the federal constitution. And the party could point to its record, which traditionally upheld programs that benefited the welfare of the family. In all, the party claimed credit for helping families by enacting legislation that ran the gamut from the Homestead Act to the Pure Food and Drug acts. For those concerned about women and children who worked in industry, the party pointed to the appropriation of funds by the Republican Congress for the Children's Bureau and the Women's Bureau in the Department of Labor.[23]

Within a week of the Republican Convention, the Democrats opened their convention in San Francisco. The Democrats more warmly received Oklahoma women delegates than the Republicans did in Chicago. Like the Republicans, the Democrats included women in the party organization before the passage of woman suffrage. In 1916 the party created a Women's Division to organize women in western states where state legislatures had passed woman suffrage amendments. By 1919 the Democrat National Committee (DNC) agreed that each state could appoint a woman associate to the committee.[24] Unlike the Republicans, the

Democrats in 1920 appointed equal representation of men and women to the Executive Committee. The more liberal attitude of the Democrats toward women in the party reflected a campaign strategy to recruit women voters into the party ranks. The goal was to portray the Democrat party as the "woman's party."

Democrat women officially organized in Oklahoma City in January 1920, when they held the first Women's Democrat Convention. State chairman of the party, Ben F. Lafayette, called the convention in hopes that women would feel included in the political organization. The chairman evidently had a secondary motive. If the women held their own convention, they would, perhaps, not feel compelled to attend the Democrat State Convention to be held in Muskogee in February. In this way, the men could keep women from meddling in party affairs. Many women resented this diversionary tactic, but ultimately, the women's convention turned out to be a huge success. What Democrat women demonstrated was that there were a significant number of women interested in the Democrat party. More than 1,000 women from around the state traveled to Oklahoma City to participate in the convention. After listening to political speakers and attending educational sessions, the women wrote resolutions that reflected their stand on political issues. Their political concern reached beyond that of home and family. The women supported President Woodrow Wilson's fight for the League of Nations. Whether the United States should join its allies in the League was a highly controversial issue that did not even have the support of many in the Democrat party. But for the most part, it was an issue that divided Democrats and Republicans and became a campaign issue in the presidential election in November 1920.[25]

The women also endorsed Oklahoma Senator Robert L. Owen for president and called for Oklahoma Democrat Governor James B. A. Robertson to hold a special session of the legislature to ratify the Susan B. Anthony Suffrage Amendment to the federal constitution. Robertson, however, was not willing to call a special session. He explained to the convention delegates that people of Oklahoma could not afford the expense of a special session, especially during a time of government frugality. Before the convention ended, the women proposed that the Oklahoma State Convention vote to send a delegation of women to accompany the men of the party to the national convention to be held in San Francisco in August 1920. This idea was as popular as the one asking the governor to call a special session on suffrage. Ultimately, however, the state

Democrats chose nine women delegates to attend the national convention. Surprisingly, there were more women than men in the Oklahoma delegation.[26] Like the Republican women, Oklahoma women in the Democrat party believed that their participation at the convention would allow them the opportunity to place measures in the party platform that addressed the welfare of women.

Oklahoma had the distinction of sending more women than any other state.[27] Journalists covering the event found the Oklahoma women interesting in that two of them were of Native American ancestry. Mrs. R. L. Fite of Tahlequah was the grandniece of Sequoyah, creator of the Cherokee alphabet.[28] Proud of her native ancestry, Fite appeared in full Cherokee regalia during her stay in San Francisco, which most likely drew the attention of more than one curious journalist looking for an interesting story. The delegation also included Roberta Campbell Lawson of Nowata, the granddaughter of Rev. Charles Journeycake, the last chief of the Delaware.[29] Besides the women delegates, there were more than twenty-eight women, many with their daughters, who made the trip to San Francisco. There was a festive air to the experience that seemed to be missing in the Republican delegation. At first the women Democrats hoped to run a special train from the Sooner State to San Francisco by way of the Grand Canyon, but they could not secure the minimum reservation of 125 people. So, instead of a special train, the ladies arranged to have four cars attached to the regular California-bound Santa Fe, the train scheduled a twenty-four-hour stop at the Grand Canyon. The delegation left June 21, arriving in San Francisco three days later. To combat heavy fog and cold winds blowing in from the Pacific, advisors warned Oklahoma women to don their fur coats and heavy jackets in preparation for their first foray into the national political arena.[30]

Myrtle Archer McDougal was leader of the Oklahoma women's delegation and a member of the Permanent Organizational Committee of the Democrat party. McDougal and the other women delegates were a part of ninety-three women delegates from across the nation who attended the convention.[31] After the Oklahoma women arrived in San Francisco, they checked into the St. Francis Hotel and then rushed off to meet with presidential candidate and Oklahoma Senator Robert L. Owen. Owen had the distinction of being one of the first senators elected to the United States Congress from the Sooner State. He was a progressive and his programs were popular with Oklahoma women.[32] He supported suffrage and worked to pass a suffrage amendment to the Oklahoma

HARLOW'S WEEKLY
A Journal of comment and current events for Oklahoma
Victor E. Harlow, Editor

June 25,1923

Oklahoma Women in Politics
By Nelle Bunyan Jennings

Democratic delegates to the national convention at San Francisco, newspaper writers and visitors filled four special cars at the Santa Fe station at Oklahoma City Monday afternoon and left at 3:55 o'clock for the west. A big crowd of friends saw the travelers on the train and assisted the late comers with getting their baggage aboard. A camera man filmed the crowd, and the comers with getting their baggage abroad. A camera man filmed the crowd and the stay at homes by the week-end will be viewing he whole proceeding on the screen of the local theater.

Mrs. Richard L. Fite of Tahlequah, state chairman of the democratic women's educational bureau, was in the capital over Sunday conferring with Mrs. John Hamill of Norman, chairman of the Fifth district educational division. Mrs. Fite had the double honor of being the first woman delegate to be named by Senator Owen and also the choice of the state convention. Mrs. Fite had with her a complete Indian costume that she will wear during her stay in San Francisco. She sill be at the Hotel Lankershiem, and following the convention will spend a few days visiting the great contralto, Mme. Schumann-Heink, at he home, Point Loma, near San Diego, immediately upon her return from the west Mrs. Fite will devote her whole time to the work of the campaign, and will be in Oklahoma City again July 15th, to preside at the conference of third district chairmen of the educational bureau. The chairmen of the bureaus in each of the 77 counties of the state will also be at this meeting.

and national constitutions. He also supported social legislation such as the Child Labor Act, the eight-hour day, and the Minimum Wage and Workman's Compensation Acts.[33] Perhaps the reason there were so many women delegates from Oklahoma was that Owen, who had considerable political influence, nominated most of the women in the delegation who attended the convention in San Francisco.

The passage of the Susan B. Anthony Suffrage Amendment to the federal constitution was not one of the key causes occupying the time of Democrat women at the convention. The women did not want suffrage to overshadow other important issues that they thought should be included in the party platform. The women believed that they had done all they could to fight for woman suffrage. It was now up to the states to ratify the nineteenth amendment. Not all women, however, were in agreement that the fight was out of their hands. Mrs. Abby Scott Baker, publicity chairman of the National Woman's Party, mounted her own campaign to convince Democrats to include a woman suffrage plank in the party platform. She announced at the convention that President Wilson had asked the Democrat governor from Tennessee to call a special session of the legislature to ratify the amendment. By so doing, Tennessee would be the thirty-sixth state to ratify it. Mrs. Baker became alarmed when the Tennessee governor balked at calling his legislature into session. He feared that there would be a backlash against himself and the Democrat party in Tennessee if his state became the final state to ratify the amendment, and therefore, was responsible for the enfranchisement of women. Mrs. Baker argued that just the opposite would occur—women would flock into the Democrat party because a Democrat state had passed the amendment. Time was of the essence for Mrs. Baker. She feared that if Tennessee did not ratify the amendment, then women would not be eligible to vote in the August presidential primaries that were scheduled in states across the South. She did not take the issue to Democrat women, but to Senator Carter Glass of Virginia, chairman of the Platform Committee. She threatened Glass that if the Democrat party did not support a suffrage plank, then women would join ranks into a third-party movement. The tactic evidently worked. Shortly after returning to her hotel from her conference with Senator Glass, she told journalists that "Senator Glass has given me his promise that there will be a suffrage plank in the Democratic platform." Similar to the Republicans, the plank on suffrage called on Democrat governors to call special sessions of their state legislatures to ratify the nineteenth amendment.[34]

47

The issues that the Democrat women believed should be included in the party platform were similar to those of Republican women. Both parties believed in legislation for the welfare of women and children. Therefore, it was important that the congress continue appropriations for the Women's Bureau in the federal government. Unlike the Republican women, the Democrat ladies supported passage of the Sheppard-Towner Bill and creation of a federal Department of Education with a director, ideally a women, who was part of the president's Cabinet.[35] The platform adopted at the Democrat Convention included many of the progressive ideals of Senator Owen and the Oklahoma women delegates. The women worked on an industrial plank that included the right to collective bargaining between employers and employees, child labor laws for children under fourteen, an eight-hour work day for women in industry, equal pay for men and women, minimum wage, federal trade commission authority over the food industry, federal and state employment offices, and creation of a voluntary labor corps for harvesting with transportation subsidies. They also recommended continued funding for the Women's Bureau. Along with their industrial plank, the women offered their support of President Wilson's League of Nations.[36]

Democrat women were more successful at being heard at the convention than the Republican women in Chicago. Again, it was most likely because of the support they received from Senator Owen. But, as successful as Mrs. McDougal and the women delegates were in working with Owen, McDougal did not have the honor of placing his name into nomination for president of the United States. It was Hadn Linebaugh of Muskogee who placed the senator's name before the Democrats. And it was Mrs. Susan W. Fritzgerald of Boston who seconded Owen's nomination. Fritzgerald had met Owen when he spoke in Massachusetts several months before the national convention. Since that time, she arranged speaking engagements for the senator throughout the East. Her support and efforts no doubt influenced the decision by Owen and the party for Mrs. Fritzgerald to participate in the nomination process. By so doing, Mrs. Fritzgerald was the first woman to speak from the platform at a Democrat National Convention. Press reports recounted that, as she walked onto the platform, the band played "You Great Big Beautiful Doll." Evidently, the sight of women on the platform was a quite a moment. One observer stated, "We confess that it gave us something of a shock to see Mrs. Fritzgerald walk out there onto that happy hunting ground of generations of men, only, looking rather as if she was calling the children home to supper."[37] Although Myrtle McDougal did not represent Oklahoma at the convention by placing Owen's name in nomination, she did have the honor of speaking from the platform when she nominated Senator Joseph T. Robinson of Arkansas as chairman of the convention. McDougal also placed in nomination General Tyson from her home state of Tennessee as the vice presidential candidate. This last honor gave McDougal the distinction of being the last person to speak from the convention platform.[38] Oklahoma women faired better at the Democrat Convention than their Republican sisters in Chicago. The DNC changed its rules to give women equal representation with men, which also would give women an equal voice in policy making. Oklahoma women also had an advantage in that they had the valuable support of Senator Owen, who was their mentor and no doubt helped influence women's activities at the convention. Also significant for Oklahoma women was that their delegation leader, Myrtle McDougal, was appointed national committeewomen for the party.

Republican and Democrat women returned to Oklahoma charged with the responsibility of educating and organizing women to work for their party's victory in the upcoming national and state elections. Their first order of business would be to convince women that it was their civic responsibility to vote. The concern was that Oklahoma women tended not to understand that with suffrage came a responsibility to get involved in politics, a sphere traditionally reserved for men and very foreign to most women. Political observers remembered that very few women took the opportunity to cast their first vote in the March 1919 election for a $50,000,000 Road Bond Bill. Low voter turnout among women caused political commentators to criticize women's apparent lack of civic duty.[39] This criticism inspired a well-organized campaign to encourage women to vote in the August 3, 1920, primary election. Taking the lead in organizing Oklahoma women to fight for the Democrat cause was Mrs. R. L. Fite, who was state chairwoman of the Democrat Women's Educational Bureau, chairwoman of the first Women's Democrat Club of Oklahoma, and chairwoman of the World War I liberty loan drive. As chairwoman of her party's educational program, she conducted a conference in Oklahoma City in July 1920. Chairmen from Oklahoma's seventy-seven counties, along with representatives from eight congressional districts, attended the meeting. They reported on their organizing efforts and perfected plans for the remaining weeks of the Democrat campaign. Each chairwoman went back to her community to develop educational programs to encourage women to take a leading role in politics, especially by voting. One of the most difficult tasks for the party was to try to dispel the belief held by many women that it was not ladylike to associate with politicians or become involved in politics, even by casting their votes. Women educators stressed that the foundation of the country revolved around politics. But perhaps an argument more germane to the sensibilities of women was that their votes would secure the welfare of their children.[40]

As the fall election moved closer, women organized Democrat clubs to better inform all women of campaign issues. At club meetings, they talked of the responsibilities of citizenship and of the new power women had through the ballot to initiate social change in the state and the country.[41] Political clubs offered women an opportunity to further their interest in politics and to educate one another about candidates running for local or national office. The clubs also helped women to rally around the party's candidates. In support of Democrat presidential candidate Governor James M. Cox of Ohio, Democrat women in Tulsa organized the first women's Cox and Roosevelt Club with thirty-one charter members. They sent a telegram to Governor Cox pledging their support. The women were confident and ambitious—their goal was to recruit five hundred members of the club in less than a week.[42] As the November election drew closer, Democrat women stepped up their campaign to recruit women into the Democrat fold. The party sent women speakers and organizers into every large city and county seat in the state to discuss the political issues of the campaign. The spokeswomen also explained the nuts and bolts of voting—how to register and mark their ballots. The meetings held across the state were also semisocial affairs. By mixing speeches with receptions and dinners, the negative connotation associated with politics had fewer rough edges.[43] Two weeks before the election, Myrtle McDougal planned a series of meetings directed at women from all political parties. The first was dubbed the "League School," a meeting to inform women on the need for the United States to join the League of Nations. There were also registration teas, held in the comfort of the home, and rallies to energize the electorate.[44]

Like the Democrat women, Republican women worked diligently to recruit women into the party and hoped to capture their votes in the fall election. After Lola Pearson returned to Oklahoma from the Republican Convention in Chicago, she joined prominent Republican women from across the country in a campaign speaking tour of the Sooner State. Newspaper accounts dubbed the Republicans as members of the "Flying Squadron" because air travel was the surest method of transporta-

HARLOW'S WEEKLY
A Journal of comment and current events for Oklahoma
Victor E. Harlow, Editor

September 17,1920

Oklahoma Women in Politics
By Nelle Bunyan Jennings

The republican women in the state officially opened their intensive speaking campaign beginning Monday of the current week. A "flying squadron" composed of seven women of national prominence in club, social, and professional circles, visited every congressional district in the state and spoke at many different points daily during the entire week

Those who visited Oklahoma, sent by the national headquarters, are Mrs. Margaret Hill McCarter of Kansas, Miss Perele Lucille Dunham of Chicago, Mrs. Sarah Sherman Maxon of Chicago, Mrs. W. W. Remington of Minneapolis, Mrs. Frank Dodson of Iowa, Mrs. Wm. Sprague of Chicago, Mrs. Robert J. Burdette of Los Angeles and Miss jean Hyde of Salt Lake City, Utah.

The speakers arrived in Oklahoma City on Monday Morning and were honor guests in the afternoon at a large reception in the ballroom of the Huckins hotel. Mrs. Clarence L. Henley of Oklahoma City, advisory board member from the Fifth District, was chairman of the reception committee.

On Monday night the women held a rally downtown, roping off a section of Main street north of the Huckins hotel, and providing seats for the audience.

The ladies spoke from an improvised platform erected on a truck and gaily decorated with bunting. There was a big crowd out to hear the distinguished speakers and they were cordially received.

Beginning Tuesday, the squadron made 75 speeches at the different cities and towns they had been scheduled to visit. Elaborate preparations were made by the republicans to entertain the visitors throughout the state.

tion to most rural Oklahoma communities. From patriotically decorated truck platforms at eighty-five gatherings, the ladies discussed the issues incorporated into the Republican platform with more than twenty-five thousand people.[45]

Republican women also organized "porch parties" at the homes of prominent state Republicans. The national Republican party encouraged women leaders in the states to organize such events to get women interested in the issues espoused by the Republican candidates. The campaign porch party originated with presidential candidate Warren Harding. It was Harding's style to greet delegations of people on his front porch in Marion, Ohio, where he spoke of his program to save the country from the apparent wreckage of Wilsonian liberalism. In his front porch appearances, Harding appeared cool, calm, and collected, which contrasted greatly with his opponent, Governor Cox of Ohio. The success of Harding's front porch appearances prompted the Republican party to encourage Oklahoma women to cash in on this successful campaign technique. The first Republican porch party was held at the home of Colonel and Mrs. Amos Ewing in September 1920. The affair was very patriotic with an orchestra and a community sing. Lecturers at the event spoke to more than two hundred women about the Republican stand on the League of Nations and social welfare legislation concerning child welfare and women in industry.[46,47] Perhaps the coup de grace of the political season for the Republican women was Mrs. Warren G. Harding's visit to the Sooner State in October 1920 while accompanying her husband on a campaign tour of the American Southwest. Her speech to Republican women at a reception held in her honor reiterated the general theme of encouraging women to vote. Mrs. Harding informed her audience that a woman could not do "her full duty toward the home unless she shows an interest in practical politics and participates in the election by voting."[48]

Oklahoma women not only believed it was their duty as citizens to participate in the electoral process, but they also thought that the state could benefit by electing women to political office. In Oklahoma, after the suffrage amendment was added to the state's constitution, it was possible for women to be elected to the state legislature and appointed to political positions throughout the state. Women could not, however, run for state office. The Oklahoma Constitution, although considered by many to be one of the most progressive of the United States, was not progressive for women. Besides restricting suffrage to males, Article V of the constitution stated that only males over thirty could run for the eight

THE DAILY OKLAHOMAN

OKLAHOMA CITY, SUNDAY, DECEMBER 5, 1920

Clerk of Harmom County Wins Senate Seat and Plans Political Future

By Vivian V. Sturgeon

Fires of determination glinting in her blue eyes, a young woman once marked off a square of hard-baked prairie soil in sand blown Harmon county. Setting her small foot upon the spade, she started to dig her own "dugout."

This was a pioneer incident of twenty years ago. The dainty young woman was a widow, the oldest of her five children was ten and she had just filed on the claim. Such work was new to her.

She dug her basement home four feet deep, lined it with boards stood on end, and she had just filed on the claim. Such work was new to her.

Then she drove her mule team thirteen miles to the red River wee she cut posts. A mule dragged into the wagon the logs she could not lift. With the posts she put up a wire fence around her quarter section of land. A part of the fence is still standing.

In blowing sand storms she "put out" a twenty-acre crop. The 10 yr. old boy helped, buckling the collars of the two mules and climbing the fence to slip them on. He guided the plow while his mother drove the mules.

Her courage is of the chilled steel variety. Through various business ventures, and tenure of several county offices she has provided for her children, reared and educated them, and watched them leave her, one by one. "I have time now to set a stone rolling for the good of humanity, if I can," she said.

January 4, 1921, Mrs. Lamar Looney of Hollis, Harmon County, will take her seat to the state senate, the fourth senatorial district sent. She expects to be admitted to the bar next year.

"There is nothing extraordinary about me, but I will tell you whatever you would like to know," she said to in interviewer this week.

Daily Oklahoman, Dec. 5, 1920

major state offices. Article V also prohibited women from jury service.[49] It was not anticipated when the states ratified the woman suffrage amendment that women would run for political office. The issue was not part of the suffrage campaign and the leaders of the suffrage movement did not officially address it. But women being elected to public office was not a foreign concept. It was common for women to run for offices associated with the school systems, particularly school superintendents, and county offices like county clerk. There were also a few women who were elected to state legislatures before final passage of the suffrage amendment. This trend continued after suffrage when there was a marked increase in the number of women running and winning seats in state legislatures.[50] The November 1920 election offered Oklahoma women their first opportunity to compete with men for national and state office. Two democrat women, Mrs. Lamar Looney of Hollis and Mrs. Daisy Coldiron of Perry, threw their bonnets into the political arena. Mrs. Looney won her seat in the Oklahoma Senate, whereas, Coldiron lost her bid for the Oklahoma House of Representatives. Unlike most politically active women, Looney did not fit the professional upper-middle-class character of many women active in politics in the 1920s. Mrs. Looney was born in Talladuga, Alabama and moved to Oklahoma in 1898. Her husband, D. T. Looney, died around 1900, leaving Looney with six children under the age of ten to raise. She taught music to make ends meet but then took up homesteading. As the story goes, Looney traded in her organ for a team of horses and filed on a quarter section of land about a mile from Hollis. At that time, Hollis was in Greer County, Texas. With the help of neighbors, Looney built a dugout, using logs from the Red River to cut handmade shingles. She left her farm and moved into Hollis in 1902 in order to provide an education for her children. She supported her family by opening a real estate office, selling insurance, and clerking in various stores in Hollis. In 1912 she was one of six candidates running for the office of Registrar of Deeds for Harmon County. Next, the voters elected Looney to the office of County Treasurer. She held the office from 1917 until 1921. Looney was also chairman of the Women's Suffrage Association for Harman County in 1918. Looney believed that her success in winning was due partly to the influence of women.[51] Others, however, viewed Looney's victory in the primary over her opponent, incumbent George L. Wilson of Mangum, as payback time for those males who worked to defeat woman suffrage. In all, six antisuffrage candidates lost in the primary election. The editor of the *Wapanucka Press* wrote, "The returns of the primary election show that it was suicidal for candidates to oppose woman suffrage." Countering this, however, was the defeated incumbent, George Wilson. The editor of the *Shawnee News* recorded Wilson's comments, "The women just decided that they were going to vote for one of their own, and I'll tell the world that they did it, he added with a smile."[52] It was assured that Looney would win the November election. The counties in her district were solidly Democrat. Looney served in the Oklahoma Senate from 1921 to 1929. Her primary motivation for running for legislative office was to help the Oklahoma farmer. She was especially interested in the quality of rural education and worked to increase legislative funding for rural schools. Looney was also supportive of women's issues and promoted measures that affected the rights of women and children.

Four Republican women filed for the Oklahoma House of Representatives. Bessie McColgin of Roger Mills County won the election in November 1920, thus becoming the first women to win a seat in the Oklahoma House.[53] Many considered McColgin a superior orator and believed her election win was do to her popularity in western Oklahoma. McColgin was a graduate of Wesleyan School of Oratory in Bloomington, Illinois. She was a former schoolteacher and the mother of eight children. The youngest was four years old when Oklahomans elected McColgin to office. Bessie McColgin only served one term in the Oklahoma House of Representatives. As a legislator she made no lasting contribution to helping Oklahoma women or the state.[54]

After suffrage, Oklahoma women in politics were seen in an altogether different manner than before suffrage when they had little political identity. In 1920 Oklahomans considered that women could be beneficial members of state government. Governor Robertson was the first to appoint a woman to a state agency when he selected Mrs. Faye L. Roblin to become a member of the State Industrial Commission. Her experience as a court reporter, law clerk, and secretary of the commission from 1917–20 made her a likely candidate. Women's clubs and labor leaders endorsed the Governor's appointment of Roblin. While serving on the commission, she studied and passed the Bar, subsequently becoming a member of the county, state, and national Bar Associations.[55] The function of the commission was to ensure the welfare of Oklahomans employed in industry; especially to see that employers carried insurance as dictated by Oklahoma law. Roblin's appointment to the commission would help the relationship between the commission and working-class women, who were especially timid about seeking help for themselves or their families.

THE DAILY OKLAHOMAN

OKLAHOMA CITY, SUNDAY, DECEMBER 5, 1920

Mother to Leave Six Children at Home When She Comes to the Capital

Mrs. Bessie McColgin, of Rankin, elected state representative from Roger Mills County, is the second of the two pioneer who will be the first women to sit in the Oklahoma Legislature.

She, like Mrs. Lamar Looney, state senator-elect, is a "self-made woman."

In 1901, with her husband, J. McColgin, and their three children, she came to Grant county, driving from there across the state to the Roger Mills County "claim" in 1908.

"I drove the team of one of our two covered wagons." She said. "The three little children were in my wagon, and on Cott Creek, west of Cheyenne, on night we hurried to cross the stream before an approaching rain storm. On a high side of my wagon wheels slipped into a deep rut and the wagon rolled slowly over, breaking an axle. Buckets of milk, water and molasses setting on the side poured their contents over the red hills and the cries of the three children broke the lonely prairie quiet.

"We went, on with one wagon through Rankin, where Uncle Tommy Ranki8n, the founder, storekeeper and postmaster could have carried all the mail in his pocket, to within a mile and a half of the Texas border, arriving at the claim after three weeks travel.

"We found a triffic prairie fire had swept the country, burning everything for miles including the little home and contents set up for us in February.

So, we began all over again, and the money saved for seed had to go for lumber to build a new home, and the strength of the teams that should have gone to put in a crop went into hauling the lumber forty-five miles from Canadian Texas."

Our horses were not acclimated and ate too much sand trying to feed off the prairie grass. When they had nearly nothing to live off of, they died.

Daily Oklahoman, Dec. 5, 1920

The thought was that working-class women would not be intimidated if they worked with a woman commissioner. As the first woman to be appointed to a state commission, Roblin caught the interest of political observers who were quick to note that she did not fit the stereotype of women in politics that was promoted by newspaper editors during the suffrage campaign. Roblin dispelled the image of the political woman as "wild-eyed, and grim-visaged." As one editor wrote, Roblin was an "extremely modest woman of quiet poise and dignity."[56]

Another first for Oklahoma women, and possibly for the nation, was the appointment by Oklahoma Attorney General, Prince Frilling, of Mrs. Kathryn Van Leuven of Okmulgee as Assistant Attorney General.[57] Van Leuven was a member of the Oklahoma Bar since 1913 and served as Assistant Attorney for Nowata County. Before suffrage, she organized the Oklahoma County Young Women's Democratic Club, which merged with the men's organization after suffrage to become the League of Young Democrats. Her appointment by Attorney General Frilling was of particular note because he was a staunch antisuffrage advocate. Many Oklahoma women surprised those who believed that women had no place in politics by demonstrating political acumen and expert ability. Mrs. Van Leuven was no exception. Frilling's admiration for Van Leuven stemmed from observing her present cases before the Oklahoma Supreme Court. He was impressed with her astute arguments and her great ability as a lawyer.[58]

Oklahoma women in politics also sought their party's nomination as presidential electors. As already stated, Roberta Campbell Lawson was one of eight women delegates who attended the Democrat National Convention in San Francisco. She was also the only woman elector nominee on the Democrat ticket in 1920. What makes Mrs. Lawson stand out from other politically active women in the 1920s is that she and her husband did not share the same political convictions. Most political observers assumed that when women could vote they would vote the same party ticket as their fathers, brothers, or husbands. Lawson proved an exception to this theory. Roberta's husband, Eugene Lawson, was a prominent Republican who many considered a good prospect for governor in the new state government.[59] *Harlow's Weekly* calculated that many of the women leaders in the Republican and Democrat parties did not share the same political affiliation as male members of their families.[60]

When the states ratified the suffrage amendment in 1920, all women citizens of the United States were allowed to vote. But the political parties little recognized black women in their efforts to capture women's votes. It was not until the Republican campaign in 1924 that black women, under the leadership of Hallie Q. Brown, past president of the National Association of Colored Women (NACW), worked full time to recruit black women into the Republican ranks.[61] There is evidence, however, that black women were involved in party politics as early as 1920. The *New York Times* reported that black women worked with white women in the party at the Chicago Convention to acquire equal representation on the Republican National Committee. But the racial makeup of the convention was not reported on per se, and perhaps would not have seemed an interesting or an unusual story to northern readers.[62] But the race question was an issue in Oklahoma politics. When Oklahoma women received the right to suffrage in 1918, it was not clear to many if this right should be extended to all women, especially black women. The Democrats, in particular, were concerned that they would lose their majority status if black women exercised their franchise. The Republican party, the party of Lincoln, had more registered blacks, especially Southern blacks, than the Democrat party in 1920. The Republican party was a minority party in Oklahoma. The Democrats were alarmed at a Republican increase in 1907, and they determined from the census returns for elections in 1907 and 1908 that Republican victories in certain counties were due to the black vote. At that time, they countered the Republican threat by amending the election laws to require a literacy test as a qualification to vote for all except those who were eligible to vote before January 1, 1866, and their descendants. Although the Republicans would benefit if they fought against such discrimination, their protests were hardly audible. Both the Democrats and Republicans feared that by allowing blacks to vote there was the possibility of black rule. The electorate passed the amendment in 1910. In 1915, however, the United States Supreme Court invalidated the amendment that became known as Oklahoma's "grandfather clause." Again, the Democrats circled the wagons—Governor Robert L. Williams called a special session of the legislature to find a way around the high court's ruling. The plan they accepted was to amend the state's election laws to require all voters to register with Democrat precinct officials. All those who were eligible to vote in 1914 were automatically registered. All others, namely blacks who could not have registered in 1914 because of the grandfather clause, only had between April 30 and May 11 of 1915 to register. In this way, the Democrats figured they could eliminate most blacks, especially if blacks did not know they had this small window of opportunity to register.[63] In

1920, the enfranchisement of blacks was once again of concern to the Democrats, especially after finding out that Republicans were registering blacks to vote in counties that were traditionally Democrat strongholds. The Democrats questioned whether it was legal to register blacks since the 1915 law left no provision for future registration other than the period between April and May of 1915.

Complicating what became known as the "Negro issue" was the black woman's vote. There were no discriminatory measures written into the amendment giving Oklahoma women the right to suffrage in 1918. But again, the Democrats used a limited registration period to discourage the registration of black women. Evidently after the passage of suffrage, women were allowed a limited period of registration before the statewide road bond election in 1919. If they did not register during the designated period, they would not be allowed to vote. This seemed to be the only opportunity for all women to activate their right to suffrage. Very few black women registered because they simply were not aware of this qualification to vote.[64] Attempts to take suffrage away from black women were prevalent throughout the South in 1920. For example, in South Carolina black women could not register until they read sections of the civil and criminal code of the state and explained to the clerk the meaning of the sections.[65]

The Democrats took a rather schizophrenic approach in their efforts to stop the Republicans from gaining further political ground. On the one hand they energized recalcitrant Democrats with the fear tactic that black political equality would lead to social equality, and therefore to black dominance. The Democrats, therefore, needed to band together and make sure they stayed in power. But on the other hand, the Democrats began to politically organize blacks in order to capture their vote and, thet hoped, defeat the Republicans. To interest blacks in the Democrat party, the political leaders formed Democrat clubs and organized a statewide convention in Tulsa in October, 1920 for black Democrats. At the convention, participants listened to speeches and wrote resolutions that supported the Democrat party platform. Also in attendance at the convention were black women, who seemed to have a less visible role than male Democrats. They were not listed as speakers or delegates, but individually they were given recognition for their work on the Reception and Entertainment Committees.[66]

Although black women did participate in Democrat party politics in Oklahoma, the majority of black women were Republicans and most political observers seemed to agree that black women would vote Republican. To organize their political activity, black women formed Republican clubs. The clubs were an extension of a network of black women's clubs, which black women leaders organized under the umbrella of the National Association of Colored Women. The organizational structure of Republican clubs was to provide political education. Mrs. Florie Pugh of Oklahoma City lectured to members at her home in the evenings on how to organize precincts and districts, and she instructed women on the duties of committee chairmen and how to get voters registered. Florie also educated clubwomen about why black people should be Republicans.[67]

Politically active Democrat women, already alarmed that they were having difficulty organizing women into the party, saw the threat of the gain in Republican strength if the Republicans captured the black women's vote.[68] To counter any benefit to the Republican party from the black women's vote, Democrats used the issue of race to bring Republican white women into the Democrat fold. As Democrat Judge Thomas Owen explained at a political rally, "What will you Republican women think if you march up to the polls and vote side by side with Negro women." Mrs. Elizabeth Hundley of Oklahoma City, organizer of Democrat women's clubs, further explained, "You can drive the Negro men from the polls, but it will be harder to do it when Negro women vote. When the election day comes, you will see Negro women riding to the polls in limousines to vote for Harding. Cannot we see every good white woman in the state going to the polls to vote the Democratic ticket?"[69]

The political contest was over in the fall of 1920 when Democrats across the country went down in defeat in the November elections. The Republican victory reflected the country's weariness with the instability caused by progressive reform and the Wilson administration's lack of peacetime initiative to solve the nation's problems. The Republican campaign to return the country to normalcy appealed to a majority of Americans and ushered in the relatively conservative era of the 1920s. Democrats in Oklahoma suffered defeat and began to lose political control of the state, which they had enjoyed since 1907. Republican victories included the election of J. W. Harreld as Oklahoma's first Republican United States Senator, Alice Robertson as the nation's second United State's Congresswoman, a Republican victory in five of the eight congressional seats, and all secondary state positions contested.[70]

The Republicans delivered a tremendous political blow to the hold Democrats had on state government. None felt it as forcibly as Myrtle Archer McDougal. She was not a new recruit to the Democrat party in 1920. As a transplanted Southerner McDougal exemplified the political character of the state's Southern residents. Her interest in civic affairs began before she moved to Sapulpa, Indian Territory, in 1904. Myrtle Archer was born into an aristocratic and literary Southern family in Marietta Springs, Mississippi, August 7, 1866. Shortly after her marriage to D. A. McDougal in 1888, the couple moved to Selmer, Tennessee, where Myrtle became editor of her husband's newspaper. After another move, this time to Savannah, Tennessee, McDougal continued her newspaper work by editing a woman's edition of the local newspaper. In Savannah, McDougal also started an amateur career in theater. Myrtle and her two children stayed in Savannah while her husband investigated the possible opportunities afforded them in Indian Territory. He subsequently opened a law office and after a year of separation, Myrtle joined her husband in Sapulpa. The McDougals' move to Indian Territory was at once a cultural adjustment. Myrtle accepted life in the frontier community by convincing other transplanted Southern women to organize a social club. This was the first of many organizations that McDougal helped to establish in her early years in Sapulpa. She ultimately organized the Sapulpa Reading Club, the Oklahoma Authors Guild, and the Current Events Club. She also taught drama and volunteered her time as a nurse. Of particular note was McDougal's success in organizing Sapulpa's women's clubs into the Indian Territory Federation of Women's Clubs. McDougal served three years as the club's first president. After statehood the Indian Territory Federation merged with the Oklahoma Federation and McDougal served another four years as president of the state organization.[71]

In 1913 Governor Lee Cruse appointed McDougal as Honorary Democratic Committeewoman. McDougal attended national conventions and participated in party activities, although unofficially. The committeewoman was a Democrat because she was Southern born and bred, the Democrat party being the majority party in the South after the Civil War. When asked why she was a Democrat, McDougal recalled, "In the old South all respectable people were Democrats. No white Republicans lived in Mississippi." She grew up in Mississippi after the Civil War, where the political environment lent itself to the impression that "all republicans in the South were corrupt." She claimed that she was a grown woman before she saw a white Republican. When her family moved to the

West, she was apprehensive to what kind of politics she would encounter in a frontier area called Indian Territory. Evidently, what she saw in Oklahoma reinforced her Southern views. The Democrat losses in 1920 alarmed McDougal. Her undaunted belief in the righteousness of her party compelled her to become an outspoken critic of Republican programs. At Democrat gatherings throughout the state in early 1920s, McDougal warned of the ruin the country faced under Republican administrations. She accused the Republican party of being the party of "the corporation, the trusts and the favored few." In her view, passage of Republican legislation and protective tariffs helped corporations and moneyed interests.[72] McDougal also held the Republicans responsible for the economic condition of the country in the immediate aftermath of World War I. Before the first World War, Wilson's economic programs to prepare America for involvement in the European conflict enhanced the economic well-being of the country. In Oklahoma the federal government encouraged farmers to expand their acreage and the production of wheat and corn. Farmers often went into debt to do so, but the high price of commodities and the European demand assured economic success. Oklahomans also benefited from the increase in oil and gas exploration. From 1917 to the end to the 1920s, Oklahoma was dotted with new oil wells and a growing demand for natural gas.[73] The war industry also spurred production of coal in eastern Oklahoma, where miners were making six dollars a day. The economic prosperity of the war years, however, was temporary. After the war, cotton, corn and wheat prices declined because supply did not meet demand. Livestock markets also diminished. Falling prices made it difficult for the farmer to pay his debt, resulting in farm foreclosures and bank failures. The economic slump after the war also affected mineral production and prices in Oklahoma. Oil prices dropped from $3.50 a barrel to $1.75 a barrel in less than a year and miners were put out of work because of the reduced need for such large coal reserves.[74] McDougal informed her audiences that when Wilson was president millions of people had jobs, but under President Harding there was large-scale unemployment. It was also her view that the economic health of the country would have been assured if America had joined the League of Nations, "Had we gone into the League of Nations and established a line of credit, this country would have seen the greatest period of prosperity any country has ever known. The corn and the wheat, the products of the loom and the factory would have flowed in a steady stream to foreign shores...."[75] To restore prosperity and integrity to the country, the people had to elect Democrats to state and national offices. It was the Democrats who were the party of the people—the party of "labor, farmers, businessmen, children, and the individual." McDougal called on women in the party to use their vote to elect Democrats. She particularity admonished women who did not vote. "Good men have gone down to defeat and bad ones have been swept into office by the votes that were never cast. Women I beseech you to remember this if you forget all else I may say."[76]

The election of 1920 ushered in a more conservative climate in American politics, where Republicans and Democrats began to move away from the Progressive reform of a decade earlier. Democrats were divided into two ideological camps: those who still championed Progressive reform and Wilsonian liberalism and those who adhered to a conservative antistatism. The first group believed in the extension of the federal government to regulate public welfare, while the other group, made up of probusiness and antiprohibitionists, believed in reversing the tide of government regulation that extended to the individual and his personal conduct.[77] The Republicans were by definition more conservative than the Democrats. Their campaign in 1920 focused on economic recovery, which they believed could be accomplished with a protective tariff, lower taxes, and more efficiency in government. The Republicans did not promote government legislation to reform society but looked to traditional methods and values as a way to solve the nation's problems.[78] While men positioned "their" political parties along a more conservative road in the 1920s, women held to their progressive ideals. And, in order to accomplish many of the political goals, women found it more efficient to establish their own political organizations where they could better influence state and national legislation. By so doing, women promoted a new progressivism that continued to shape the political dialogue throughout the 1920s.

NOTES

1. *Harlow's Weekly*, 19 November 1919.
2. Robert K. Murray, *The Politics of Normalcy: Governmental Theory and Practice in the Harding-Coolidge Era*, (New York: W. W. Norton, 1973), pp. 4–9.
3. For an analysis of women's participation in politics after 1920, the following studies are helpful: Kristi Anderson, *After Suffrage: Women in Partisan and Electoral Politics Before the New Deal*, (Chicago: University of Chicago Press, 1996); Kristi Anderson, "Women and Citizenship in the 1920s," in Louise A. Tilly and Patricia Gurin, *Women, Politics, and Change*, (New York: Russell

Sage Foundation, 1990); Nancy F. Cott, "Across the Great Divide: Women in Politics Before and After 1920," in Louise A. Tilly and Patricia Gurin, *Women, Politics, and Change*, (New York: Russell Sage Foundation, 1990); Nancy Cott, *The Grounding of Modern Feminism*, (New Haven: Yale University Press, 1987); Melanie Gustafson, ed., *We Have Come to Stay: American Women and Political Parties, 1880–1960*. (University of New Mexico Press, 1999).

4. *Harlow's Weekly*, 11 June 1920; Official Program of the Republican National Convention, June 8, 1920, Lola Clark Pearson Collection, Western History Archive, University of Oklahoma, Norman, Oklahoma. Hereafter cited LCP.

5. In all there were 984 women delegates attending the convention. Josephine L. Good, *The History of Women in Republican National Conventions and Women in the Republican National Committee*, (Washington, D.C.: Republican National Committee, 1963), pp. 9, 11.

6. Anderson, *After Suffrage*, p. 92.

7. James J. McGraw to Mrs. J. C. Pearson, 4 May 1920, LCP.

8. Harriet E. Vittum to Mrs. J. C. Pearson, 18 May 1920, LCP.

9. *Harlow's Weekly*, 11 June 1920, 21 June 1920.

10. Good, *The History of Women in Republican National Conventions and Women in the Republican National Committee*, pp. 11–12.

11. *New York Times*, 31 May 1920; Anderson, *After Suffrage*, p. 81.

12. The breakdown of the vote in the United States House and Senate was 91 percent of the House Republicans voted to pass the amendment while 40 percent of the Democrats did not. In the Senate the numbers were similar; 81 percent of the Republican voted yes while only 45 percent of the Democrats did. Also interesting is that twenty-nine of the thirty-six states who eventually ratified the amendment had Republican legislatures. Of those states that refused to ratify, eight were Democrats and one was Republican. Good, *The History of Women in Republican National Conventions and Women in the Republican National Committee*, pp. 5, 8, 9.

13. *New York Times*, 4 June 1920.

14. Good, *The History of Women in Republican National Conventions and Women in the Republican National Committee*, p. 13.

15. *New York Times*, 9 June 1920.

16. J. Stanley Lemons, *The Woman Citizen Social Feminism in the 1920s*, (Urbana: University of Illinois Press, 1973), pp. 25–30.

17. Good, *The History of Women in Republican National Conventions and Women in the Republican National Committee*, p. 13. In 1920 the Congress appropriated $75,000 for a permanent Women's Bureau. Women ultimately used the bureau as an agency to fight for equal pay, equal job opportunity, and for

equality in promotion and training. Lemons, *The Woman Citizen*, pp. 25–30.

18. Ibid, pp. 63–65.
19. *New York Times*, 9 June 1920.
20. More will be said on Sheppard-Towner Maternity and Infancy Bill in subsequent chapters.
21. Lemons, *Woman Citizen*, pp. 129–130.
22. *Seventeenth Republican National Convention*, Chicago, 1920, (New York: Tenny Press, 1920), p. 108.
23. *The Woman, the Child and the Republican Party*, (Washington, D.C.: Republican National Committee, 1922.
24. Andersen, *After Suffrage*, pp. 81–85.
25. *New York Times*, 11 June 1920.
26. *Harlow's Weekly*, 28 January 1920.
27. *New York Times*, 26 June 1920.
28. Mrs. R. L. Fite was born in Indian Territory. She was a graduate of the Cherokee Female Seminary, the wife of Dr. Richard L. Fite, and the mother of four children. She was politically allied with prominent Oklahoma Democrats. Among her political acquaintances were State Chairman of the Democrat party, Ben F. Lafayette, and Governors M. E. Trapp, J. B. A. Robertson, and W. J. Holloway. Harlow, *Makers of Government in Oklahoma*, p. 82.
29. Roberta Campbell Lawson was born in Al-lu-ne, Indian Territory. She attended Hardin College, Mexico, Missouri. She was married to Eugene B. Lawson. The couple had one child. Lawson was an active clubwoman with memberships in the National Women's Democrat Club, Washington, D.C., the DAR, the Daughters of 1812, and was 2nd vice-president of the General Federation of Woman's Clubs. She was also a Trustee of the University of Tulsa, and a member of the Board of Regents of Oklahoma College for Women in Chickasha. During the first World War, Lawson was State Chairman for the Women's Committee of the National Council of Defense. Roberta's civic endeavors in Nowata included organizing the first women's club and establishing a park and public library. Harlow, *Makers of Government in Oklahoma*, p. 787.
30. *Harlow's Weekly*, 11 June 1920.
31. Andersen, *After Suffrage*, p. 83; *New York Times*, 26 June 1920.
32. *New York Times*, 26 June 1920
33. Robert Owen was a southern progressive who migrated to Oklahoma before statehood. Owen settled in Indian Territory where he taught school until appointed by President Grover Cleveland as Superintendent of Union Agency at Muskogee. He was active in Democrat party affairs in Indian Territory and

gained some political advantage from his Cherokee ancestry. Owen's mother was one-eighth Cherokee. *Daily Oklahoman,* 1 July 1920.

34. *New York Times,* 28 June 1920.

35. Ibid.

36. *New York Times,* 26 June 1920.

37. *Daily Oklahoman,* 1 July 1920.

38. *Harlow's Weekly,* 15 November 1920.

39. In towns where there were low turnouts of women voters, there were corresponding low numbers of male voters. Evidently, in rural areas of the state, there was little excitement over most of the issues on the primary ballot. In the larger urban areas, however, there were hotly debated contests that drew a significant number of men and women to the polls. *Harlow's Weekly,* 2 April 1920.

40. *Harlow's Weekly,* 25 June 1920; 16 July 1920.

41. *Harlow's Weekly,* 27 August 1920.

42. *Harlow's Weekly,* 23 July 1920.

43. *Harlow's Weekly,* 24 September 1920.

44. *Harlow's Weekly,* 15 October 1920, 22 October 1920.

45. *Harlow's Weekly,* 24 September 1920.

46. The Republicans did not believe that the Versailles Treaty championed by Wilson would accomplish world peace. Instead, the party believed that the treaty set the stage for conflict and controversy among nations. It was the Republican plan that when peace was threatened, the "decision of impartial courts" could call an international conference where those nations who pledged to keep international peace would use their influence and power for the prevention of war. Although the Republican plan did not seem all that different than the concept of a League of Nations as proposed by Wilson, members of the Republican party believed that their plan could be accomplished without a compromise to national independence; United States troops could not be called by an international body to settle disputes among fighting nations.

47. *Harlow's Weekly,* 10 September 1920.

48. *Harlow's Weekly,* 15 October 1920.

49. Janice P. Dreiling, "Women and Oklahoma Law: How It Has Changed, Who Changed It, and What is Left," *Oklahoma Law Review,* 1987.

50. Anderson, *After Suffrage,* p. 111; Cott, *Grounding of Modern Feminism,* p. 100.

51. *Harlow's Weekly,* 14 April 1922; Harlow, *Makers of Government in Oklahoma,* p. 243.

52. Quoted in *Harlow's Weekly,* 27 August 1920.

53. Bessie S. McColgin was born in Minneapolis, Kansas, in 1875. After graduating from high school in Earlville, Illinois, she attended Teachers Normal College and Wesleyan University in Bloomington, Illinois. Her education also included the School of Oratory and Georgian Academy in Georgia, Vermont. Her husband was Grant McColgin, farmer and stockman. The McColgin's had eight children. She was an active member of the Women's Missionary Society and Ladies Aid Society. She also belonged to the Grange and the 4-H club, and she was one of the organizing members of the Farmer's Union. Harlow, *Makers of Government in Oklahoma*, p. 714.

54. Directory of Oklahoma, 1989–1990 State Almanac; *Harlow's Weekly*, April 1922.

55. *Harlow's Weekly*, 11 June 1920, 18 June 1920; Faye L. Roblin was born in Minneapolis, Minnesota, in 1886. She moved to Guthrie, Oklahoma, in 1891. She obtained her education at Buffalo University in New York, where she studied music. Her political associations included ex-Democrat governors Robert L. Williams, M. E. Trapp and W. J. Holloway. Harlow, *Makers of Government in Oklahoma*, p. 573.

56. *Harlow's Weekly*, 18 June 1920.

57. Kathryn Van Leuven was born in Fort Smith, Arkansas, in 1888. She moved to Oklahoma in 1906 and resided in Tahlequah, Muskogee, and Nowata before moving to Oklahoma City in 1914. She graduated from high school in Arkansas and attended "special" classes at the University of Chicago (most likely law classes). She was admitted to the Oklahoma bar in 1913. Her husband was Judge Bert Van Leuven; the couple had one child. Harlow, *Makers of Government in Oklahoma*, p. 590.

58. *Harlow's Weekly*, 27 August 1920.

59. Eugene Lawson was a Kentuckian who moved to Indian Territory to practice law. The Lawson's eventually became civic and financial leaders in Nowata, where the couple managed to make a fortune in the oil business. Marion E. Gridley, *American Indian Women*, (New York: Hawthorn Books, 1974), pp. 88–93; New York Times, 6 June 1920; *Harlow's Weekly*, 25 June 1920, 1 November 1920, 26 November 1920.

60. *Harlow's Weekly*, 1 October 1920.

61. Anderson, *After Suffrage*, p. 84.

62. *New York Times*, 7 June 1920.

63. Danny Goble, *Oklahoma Politics: A History*, (Norman: University of Oklahoma Press, 1982), pp.46, 84.

64. *Harlow's Weekly*, 1 October 1920.

65. *Black Dispatch*, 22 October 1920.

66. *Harlow's Weekly*, 8 October 1920.

67. Evelyn Brooks Higgenbotham, "In Politics to Stay: Black Women Leaders and Party Politics in the 1920s" in Louise A. Tilly and Patricia Gurin, eds., *Women, Politics, and Change*, (New York: Russell Sage Foundation, 1990), p. 208.

68. *Harlow's Weekly*, 1 October 1920.

69. *Harlow's Weekly*, 8 October 1920.

70. Bureau of Government Research, Western History Collection, University of Oklahoma, Norman, Oklahoma.

71. Mary McDougal Axelson, "Her Hands: In Remembrance of Myrtle Archer McDougal," Mary McDougal Axelson Collection, Archives and Special Collections, University of Miami, Coral Gables, Florida.

72. Myrtle Archer McDougal, Speech, Mary McDougal Axelson Collection, Archives and Special Collections, University of Miami, Coral Gables, Florida.

73. Paul Bonnifield, *The Dust Bowl, Men, Dirt, and Depression*, (Albuquerque: University of New Mexico Press, 1979), pp. 20–38.

74. H. Wayne Morgan and Anne Hodges Morgan, *Oklahoma, A History*, (New York: W. W. Norton, 1977), pp. 102–103.

75. Myrtle Archer McDougal, Speech, Mary McDougal Axelson Collection, Archives and Special Collections, University of Miami, Coral Gables, Florida.

76. Ibid.

77. Douglas B. Craig, *After Wilson: The Struggle for the Democratic Party, 1920–1934*, (Chapel Hill: University of North Carolina Press, 1992), p. 3.

78. Robert K. Murray, *The Politics of Normalcy: Governmental Theory and Practice in the Harding-Coolidge Era*, (New York: Norton, 1972), p. 2.

Political Action Groups
and Ideological Alignment

Politically active women in Oklahoma started the decade of the 1920s charged with the responsibility of fulfilling their duties as citizens. Anna Korn, conservative leader in the Oklahoma Democrat party, believed that the best way to do this was to organize a Women's Legislative Council. She informed women that "Living as we are in an age when woman's work and woman's influence are recognized as powerful factors in every phase of human activity, it is of primary importance that we take an interest in our government. Every woman who fails to follow the business of our legislative halls as closely and intelligently as she can is not properly fulfilling her duty of citizenship."[1] Korn was one of many Oklahoma women in the 1920s who expanded her activities to include work in political organizations, where they concentrated mainly on legislation that benefited women and the family. These political action groups reflected women's conservative or progressive philosophy on the role of government in American life. In Oklahoma, women's membership in three organizations, the Women's Legislative Council (WLC), the National League of Women Voters (NLWV) and the National Woman's Party (NWP), provides insight into women's political philosophy and its place on the ideological spectrum in the early 1920s.

The Women's Legislative Council was perhaps the most conservative women's lobbying group in Oklahoma in 1920. The Oklahoma council was one of many in the United States where women organized to coordinate legislative activities. California women established the first WLC in 1911. The idea caught on and became a force in promoting legislation in most states by the early 1920s. State organizations of the WLC were most likely patterned after the Women's Joint Congressional Committee (WJCC), a national organization whose purpose was to lobby congressional lawmakers to initiate legislation for the welfare of women. More

69

than ten million women from various women's organizations belonged to the WJCC.[2] The Women's Legislative Council in Oklahoma served the same purpose as the WJCC. Women representing the concerns of various women's clubs in Oklahoma worked through the WLC to initiate state instead of federal legislation to solve community problems. The bipartisan organization stated its purpose as a political agency whose members would "select, endorse, promote, or oppose legislative bills for the betterment of humanity in general, women and children especially." Delegates represented nonsectarian, nonpolitical women's clubs in Oklahoma, including women from the Oklahoma General Federation of Women's Clubs (consisting of 297 Oklahoma clubs), Young Women's Christian Association (YWCA), Women's Christian Temperance Union (WCTU), Daughters of the American Revolution (DAR), United Daughters of the Confederacy, and the PEO, a secret literary club.[3]

The conservative nature of the council's membership was, perhaps epitomized by Anna Korn. The councilwoman was active in Oklahoma politics, serving as vice-chairman of the Canadian County Democrat Central Committee and a member of the National Congressional Campaign Committee from 1922 to 1924. Besides her work in the Democrat party, Korn belonged to patriotic organizations that philosophically moved to the right during the 1920s. The Democrat leader was state parliamentarian of the Oklahoma division of the United Daughters of the Confederacy. Her roles in other patriotic organizations included organizer and regent of the Daughters of the American Revolution, and organizer and state president of the United States Daughters of the War of 1812. Korn's conservative roots were also in her club associations, especially her membership in the Eastern Star, the women's auxiliary to the Masons, whose membership was reported to have ties to the Oklahoma Ku Klux Klan.[4]

The conservative nature of the WLC's legislative program was apparent from the first official meeting of the council. In December 1920, before Oklahoma's eighth legislature convened, delegates of the WLC met in Oklahoma City at the Woman's Clubhouse to finish the official organization of the council. The meeting also was a strategy session on how to promote needed legislation. Women decided to put their efforts behind key social legislation that they believed had a good chance of becoming law. They were cautiously conservative about initiating legislation that expanded state government. Instead, women recommended supporting laws that were already on the statute books, such as laws on compulsory

HARLOW'S WEEKLY

A Journal of comment and current events for Oklahoma

Victor E. Harlow, Editor

December 15,1923

Oklahoma Women in Politics
By Nelle Bunyan Jennings

The big event of the week was the meeting of the Legislative Council at Oklahoma City. This Council whose membership is composed of representatives of women's organizations is just one year old being rather hurriedly perfected last year before the Legislature convened. The meeting Wednesday was of utmost importance with a state election less than one year away. New officers were elected and the delegates from the different organizations presented their legislative programs. These tentative measures will all be considered at a meeting of the executive board to be held after the first will be determined upon. The Legislative Council believes that the most far-reaching work is soon to be before the women of Oklahoma, that is the spring caucuses. It is proposed that the program will be determined upon early and the candidates will then be asked to express themselves concerning these measure long enough before the primaries that every woman voter can know just how the man she is casting her ballot for or against has pledged himself to vote for the measures that the women feel are needed to vitalize many of he statues now in existence.

The very biggest thing that the women propose to do is to launch a movement to take Oklahoma schools "out of politics." Practically every woman present at the meeting stated that the men in her community have expressed themselves as believing that is the paramount and the most vital thing that the women can do this coming year. It will still be worth while if only sentiment toward this end is created during the next year. There was much talk during the last legislature about this very thing, during the time that the district Federations were holding their spring meetings and wiring the solons and passing resolutions asking this and that appropriation for the state schools, the university in particular.

education, prohibiting child labor, an eight-hour day for women in industry, vital statistics, quarantine regulations, and the age of consent. Women
believed that they only had to amend some of these laws and make the
public aware of existing laws to ensure good government.[5]

Council members did not believe that government should be completely un-responsive to the needs of society, especially in matters of improved health care for women and children. At the national level, women
promoted federal legislation for improved health care, but the women in
the WLC preferred state legislation. Council members wrote new legislation for a $25,000 appropriations bill to create a Bureau of Child Welfare
in state government and a department at the University of Oklahoma
to conduct research on nutrition, eugenics, genetics, educational child
psychology, and physical measurement. Women also supported a Bureau
of Public Health Nursing in the State Department of Health and appropriations for a full-time county health physician and public health nurse.[6]
Oklahoma had forty public health nurses in the state who were employed
by various private organizations or by larger municipalities. The creation
of a Bureau of Public Health Nursing would expand health care to each
county, where a nurse would take care of tubercular patients, provide instruction on infant care and feeding, and assist with public school health
matters. The county nurse would also help to detect physical defects in
children and see that the parents obtain necessary medical attention.[7]

As ambitious as women were in promoting useful legislation, the
lawmakers passed few of the council's proposals. Out of fourteen bills
sponsored by the WLC in 1920, only two became law—an eight-hour
workday for women in industry and a legislative act declaring November
16 Oklahoma Day.[8] Before suffrage, women had very little recourse when
legislators turned a deaf ear to women's political concerns. After ratification of the nineteenth amendment, however, women were equipped to
oppose those who did not support their legislation. Women delegates
could work to defeat recalcitrant legislators. At the April 1921 meeting
of the WLC in Alva, Oklahoma, Mrs. John H. Riehl, president of the
council, called on the delegates to censure members of the eighth legislature who demonstrated little interest in the council's legislative recommendations.[9] Women devised a plan of action against those in the ninth
legislature who did not sponsor the council's legislation. The idea was to
present their program to the lawmakers far enough in advance of the fall
elections so that women could determine which legislators were interested in promoting their concerns. If a legislator did not pledge to vote

for the council's measures, then women worked to defeat the candidate in the state election.[10]

In 1921 council members pressed forward with a new legislative program. One of the more important issues that they worked on was a proposal to amend the state constitution that gave lawmakers authority to allocate funds for Oklahoma schools. Women considered this system to be too political and believed that Oklahoma school children suffered as a result. They recommended a revision of the constitution to allow funding by a special tax levy. Other laws thought important by council members were a law that would punish those who bought liquor as well as those who sold it, a law that would provide an endowment for mothers with dependent children, a law that would impose a more severe penalty for wife abandonment—making the father responsible for dependent children until the age of sixteen, and a law that would provide independent citizenship for women.[11] Women were not any more successful in seeing their legislation voted into law during the ninth legislature than they were in the previous session. Again the lawmakers only passed two bills promoted by the council: legislation making wife and child abandonment a felony instead of a misdemeanor and a referendum for an amendment to the state constitution for a tax levy for Oklahoma schools.[12] By the mid-twenties, it was evident that Oklahoma legislators were too fiscally conservative to provide funds to expand social services in Oklahoma. Women were also fiscally conservative, but in matters concerning the well-being of the family, they promoted a progressive program. The council fought for legislation to appropriate funds to expand health care facilities in the state, particularly money for maternity and child hygiene. In legislators' quest to reduce state bureaucracy, they denied funding. A bill to provide medical care for maternity and infants was pending in the U.S. Congress in 1921. Women's groups across the country, including in Oklahoma, supported the national legislation. Since Oklahoma state legislators were not receptive to the creation or expansion of social programs, the only recourse for many of the state's progressive-minded women was to support the work of women's groups who did champion national social welfare legislation. In Oklahoma the League of Women Voters (LWV) offered women a progressive platform from which to support federal programs that provided support for health care and aided women and children in the work force.

The National League of Women Voters was formed during the final stages of the campaign for woman suffrage. In 1917 Carrie Chapman Catt, president of the National American Woman Suffrage Association

(NAWSA), outlined a plan to unite women in states where suffrage had already passed into a national league of women voters to better coordinate the fight for a federal suffrage amendment. The league became more formalized in March 1919 when suffrage supporters met in St. Louis to commemorate the fiftieth anniversary of the first state to grant suffrage to women (Wyoming). At the meeting, women accepted Catt's plan for a united suffrage organization and officially inaugurated the National League of Women Voters. The purpose of the organization was to teach women good citizenship and voter responsibility.[13] Women in the NLWV also believed that they had a social responsibility to see to the welfare of women and children, a responsibility that followed a tradition set down by nineteenth-century reformers. During the era of transition from a rural agricultural society to a more urban industrial world, middle-class women became involved in various reforms to better the lives and working conditions of women and children employed in industry. Through their reform work, it became acceptable for women to leave their domestic sphere and assume a public and political role outside the home. In so doing, women opened up the public discourse to include social issues, which were traditionally nonpolitical. Ultimately women's activism in Progressive Era reform advanced a new definition concerning the role of the government in American life. Women introduced into the political arena the ideals of a welfare state, which promoted legislation to protect the lives and well-being of women and children.[14] Women in the league continued the work of those who forged the field of reform in the nineteenth century.

After the official founding of the NLWV in St. Louis in 1917, league delegates elected Miss Katharine Pierce of Oklahoma City as secretary of the national organization.[15] Even though an Oklahoma woman was involved in the establishment of the NLWV at the national level, the beginning of the organization in Oklahoma was at first difficult. National leaders, however, were persistent in establishing branches of the league in each state in order to harmonize better promotion of league issues. In August 1920 league representative Miss Lola Walker of Pittsburgh, Pennsylvania, arrived in Oklahoma to establish a state organization before the November 1920 election. Walker's efforts were a failure. After the fall election, Miss Marie B. Ames of St. Louis tried her hand at establishing a league in Oklahoma. Her more successful approach was to operate citizenship schools that discussed the issues supported by the league. The schools helped to advertise the NLWV and to acquaint Oklahoma women with the concepts of the organization. By December of 1920, there was a

HARLOW'S WEEKLY
A Journal of comment and current events for Oklahoma
Victor E. Harlow, Editor

January 14, 1921

Oklahoma Women in Politics
By Nelle Bunyan Jennings

In her addresses to the women of Muskogee and Tulsa, Mrs. George Gellhorn of St. Louis, national vice chairman for the League of Women Voters, referred to the organization now being perfected in the state as "the new baby." Oklahoma was spoken of is this manner because it is the last state in the union to enter the national organization. That the "new Baby" is not being as cordially welcomed as was expected by its sponsors is very apparent from the following editorial that appeared during the week in the Tulsa World:

Two ideas are seeking to influence the newly enfranchised woman vote. One of them, put forth by "The League of Woman Voters," seeks to form a class-conscious voting mass that will function from the standpoint of sex citizenship. Inevitable such practice will array the woman vote in hostility to men and men in hostility to women.

The other idea, advocated in Oklahoma by Mrs. Otis Cureton, vice-chairman of the republican state committee, seeks to have the women simply function as citizens regardless of sex and in their natural alliance with existing partisan organizations. The tendency of this practice would be to make women stand on a precise equality with men and without arousing the slightest sex or class consciousness or engendering any hostility between the sexes in political matters.

Surely the thoughtful woman cannot hesitate as to her choice between these two conflicting ideas. There is not a student of politics or statecraft in the land but has unhesitatingly condemned the idea of women forming a separate party along sex lines. For them to demand recognition simply on sex ground is for them to justify all that was ever said by opponents of equal suffrage and to create a positive menace in the body politic.

There is no filed for the League of Women Voters in Oklahoma, and we prophesy that the efforts of its organizers will be fruitless among that splendid class of women who functioned so magnificently and patriotically during the last campaign, and who are content to assume their positions on the firing line of politics as citizens proud to stand shoulder to shoulder with their men, instead of Amazons ambitiously seeking a command on sex-grounds alone.

fledgling LWV organization headquartered in Muskogee, with Mrs. Phil Brown presiding as state president. Brown established eight committees in the state league, and in keeping with the nonpartisan tradition, Brown appointed four Republicans and four Democrats as committee chairmen. The committees were similar to those found in the other women's clubs in Oklahoma: committees on American citizenship, protection of women in industry, child welfare, improvement of election laws, unification of laws concerning the civil status of women, and social hygiene. Three issues were of primary concern to the Oklahoma league: passage of national legislation for the health care for women and infants during and after childbirth, an eight-hour day for women, and an amendment to the state constitution that would allow women to hold state office.[16]

There was significant opposition to the league in Oklahoma by both partisan and nonpartisan groups. To many, the LWV was not necessary because both Republican and Democrat parties, and the Women's Legislative Council, had already established schools to educate women about good citizenship and their responsibility as new voters. Mrs. Otis Cureton, vice-chairman of the Oklahoma Republican State Committee, believed, as others did, "that the leaders of the NLWV were creating a class-conscious voting mass that will function from the standpoint of sex citizenship." Cureton reasoned that gender had nothing to do with women's citizenship and that women and men had equal responsibility in party politics. Chiming in on Cureton's side, the editor of the *Tulsa World* wrote, "There is no field for the League of Women Voters in Oklahoma," and that the organizers would not be able to enlist Oklahoma women. He saw no need for a separate political organization for women because Oklahoma women already knew how to organize and work actively in politics. He pointed to women who worked in the 1920 campaign and elaborated on how they worked "magnificently and patriotically during the last campaign" and therefore, stood "shoulder to shoulder with their men, instead of Amazons ambitiously seeking a command on sex-grounds alone."[17]

The slow growth of the league in Oklahoma hindered the organization's efforts to promote their legislative agenda to Oklahoma lawmakers. In the eighth legislature in 1921, the only measure promoted by the LWV was the creation of a Women's Bureau in the Oklahoma Department of Labor. When the bill finally passed the Oklahoma House of Representatives in the summer of 1921, labor commissioner Claude Connally appointed Miss Cora Smith of Oklahoma City as head of the bureau. Smith was a former secretary of the State Board of Vocational Education and state chairman of the Committee of Women and Industries of the League of Women Voters. The bureau had a similar charge as the Women's Bureau in the federal government's Department of Labor. Smith's duties were to inspect the working conditions in factories and stores for violation of the state laws governing women and children in industry.[18]

Oklahoma women who belonged to the Women's Legislative Council or the League of Women Voters basically shared the same concern for the welfare of women and children. They sought legislation, through their respective organizations, that improved the condition of the working class and the general welfare of all women in the United States. Where these women differed was in their philosophy about state or federal action on social welfare issues. For the most part, the two groups were not that far apart in their concern for women and children and most likely their membership in the two organizations overlapped. A more radical women's political action group in Oklahoma was the National Woman's Party (NWP), whose membership at the national and local levels moved the philosophical discussion far left of center by their revolutionary call for federal government legislation on women's equality.

The National Woman's Party was formed when radical suffragist Alice Paul broke away from the NAWSA in 1914 to organize what she believed to be a more effective group in fighting for woman suffrage, the Congressional Union for Women's Suffrage (CU). Instead of winning suffrage with a state-by-state campaign as recommended by the leaders of the NAWSA, members of the CU worked at the federal level lobbying members of Congress, picketing the White House, and in an unladylike manner for the era, bringing attention to their cause by chaining themselves to the White House fence. Members of the CU also fought for feminist reform and controversial women's issues, such as birth control.[19] CU members became involved in party politics, through which they tried to use political leverage over congressmen to realize their reform goals. In 1916 the CU became the Woman's Party and, after final passage of the suffrage amendment, the National Woman's Party. Women in the National Woman's Party were hard-core feminists who believed that women's condition could only change for the better if women shared total equality with men. After suffrage, women in the NWP put most of their energy behind an amendment to the federal constitution, which guaranteed equal rights for women.[20]

Who's Rocking the Cradle?

After Alice Paul broke away from the NAWSA to establish the National Woman's Party, her plan was to organize a branch of the party in each state. In 1920 the organization in Oklahoma was small, having few if any dedicated members. The national organization appointed Ida F. Halsey of Oklahoma City as state chairman. Political commentators viewed Halsey as an "active suffragist" who placed her financial interest before her political. For example, when Alice Paul wrote Halsey that she might need her to help convince the Tennessee legislature to ratify the federal suffrage amendment, Halsey indicated that she needed to tend to the business of her oil leases and would only help if "unexpected conditions arise."[21] As it turned out, the Tennessee legislature ratified the amendment without Halsey's help. In November 1920 the state chairman called party members to meet in Oklahoma City to choose delegates to the February 1921 NWP convention in Washington, D.C. Women elected five delegates. Among them were two future state representatives to the Oklahoma legislature, Mrs. Emma Estill Harbour[22] of Edmond and Mrs. Anna Laskey of Oklahoma City.[23] At the convention, Alice Paul announced her goals for the future of the National Woman's Party. But delegates from all across the United States arrived at the convention hoping to address the assembly and present their own organizations' proposals for legislative action. Among the varied interests were representatives from pacifist groups, birth control advocates, the National Association of Colored Women, and the National Association for the Advancement of Colored People. Representatives from these organizations all vied for a place on the program so they could introduce their agendas to the assembly. But Alice Paul and top officials of the party held fast to their proposals. The thought was that to allow such issues as birth control, civil rights, or world disarmament into the party would weaken the feminist goal of fighting for women's equality.[24] By the time of the NWP national convention in 1921, there was a growing animus by Oklahomans toward the Woman's Party. The editor of the women's column in Harlow's Weekly expounded on how there was so little work for the party in Oklahoma, especially if the focus of the group's activity was on women's equal rights. Many Oklahomans evidently believed that when women won the right to suffrage, they also acquired equal citizenship under the law. This was not the case. But as the editor believed, "There is little work for the party in this state. There is little that the law offers here to a man that is not given a woman."[25]

Membership increased in the Woman's Party in Oklahoma when the national party appointed Florence Etheridge Cobb as state chairman in 1922. Cobb was an advocate and dedicated champion of women's equality. She was born in Bridgeport, Connecticut, September 20, 1878. After finishing high school in Everett, Massachusetts, she attended Washington College of Law, receiving her bachelor of law degree in 1911 and her master's degree in 1912. Two years later, Cobb was admitted to practice law before the Supreme Court of the United States. After moving to Oklahoma in 1918, Cobb became United States Probate Attorney in Vinita and was admitted to practice law before the Oklahoma Supreme Court. Throughout Cobb's professional life in Oklahoma, she was active in judicial affairs. After accepting the chairmanship of the Woman's Party, her first order of business was to investigate the legal status of Oklahoma women.[26]

Cobb's study of the Oklahoma Constitution revealed that state laws placed women in a subservient role to men. By continuing the established precedent of designating the male as the head of the family, as was the practice under English Common Law, women did not enjoy the same rights as men. Women did not share the same property rights as their husbands and they did not have custody rights of their children. Men defended this arrangement with the analysis that "Someone must be for legal reasons declared the head of the house, that is agreed, and the title is an empty one so far as honors are concerned and carries an additional responsibility besides by making the 'head' liable for debts of the family and other similar 'privileges.'"[27] Besides laws that discriminated against married women, the Oklahoma Constitution also prohibited women from holding state office and serving on juries. In cooperation with the leaders of the National Party, Florence Cobb wrote legislation that would eliminate sex discrimination in Oklahoma. But most important to her and the National Party was legislation on equal rights for women. It was the granddaddy of women's legislation and the most difficult to get anyone to sponsor.

Cobb's strategy in promoting NWP legislation was to find the right legislator as a sponsor. Recognizing that perhaps a woman would be their best ally in promoting women's concerns, Mrs. Cobb called on Oklahoma's only woman Senator, Mrs. Lamar Looney from Hollis. Looney was mildly interested in NWP legislation and only agreed to sponsor one of their bills calling for equal pay and equal opportunity. Amending the state constitution so that women were eligible to hold state office was promoted by

THE DAILY OKLAHOMAN

OKLAHOMA CITY, FRIDAY, FEBRUARY 2, 1923

HOUSE REPAIRS ANTI-KLAN ACT THEN BEATS IT

Brydia Measure Finds Only Three Supporters When Brought to Vote

---

LASKEY BANK BILL DEAD

Caddo Man Says He Can Show Where Bill Originated From Soviet Book

---

Resurrected for a moment when an amendment was adopted restoring it to its original form, the Brydia "anti-Ku klux Klan" bill was defeated on a record roll call Thursday when the house voted 93 to 3 to definitely kill the bill

Anna Laskey's bill to establish a state owned bank as a depository for publick funds had been killed a few moments before the roll call demanded by the leaders showing the result of 83 to 12.

Three Supported Bill

The so-called Klan bill, house bill 132, came up under regular order, requiring the registration of memberships by all secret organizations and aimed to be the Ku Klux Klan, according to its author, Fred F. Brydia of Pontotoc, although amended Wednesday to exclude from its provision members of farm and labor organizations and the klan.

Brydia, with unanimous consent offered an amendment restoring the bill to its original from. This was adopted with but few dissenting votes and opponents of the bill then united in demand for a record bote. Edyth Mitchell of Payne, W. H. Case of Okfuskee and Brydia, alone supported the bill on the final roll call.

Daily Oklahoman, Feb, 02, 1923

most politically active women in Oklahoma, and Looney had already prepared a bill to introduce to the legislature. Looney proposed that the word
"male" be replaced with the word "citizen," in the state constitution.[28]
Cobb was disappointed that Looney would not sponsor the National
Woman's Party legislation on women's equality. Cobb wrote to the national headquarters that Looney was "inclined to be hesitant in the matter of what I consider our most important measure, namely the blanket
equality bill."[29] Leaders in the party suggested to Cobb that she should ask
Anna Laskey, state representative from Oklahoma County and a member
of the National Woman's Party, to sponsor NWP legislation. Cobb had
initially considered Laskey, but politically, Cobb understood that Laskey's
activities on behalf of the Socialist party might prejudice people against
women's legislation. As a member of the state house, Anna Laskey tried to
"sponsor all humanitarian and progressive legislation," especially legislation for the welfare of the farmer and laborer. But she was also interested
in women obtaining their political rights and enjoying equal citizenship
with men. Laskey became active in Oklahoma politics before statehood
as a promoter of woman suffrage. Her appeal for suffrage emanated from
her belief that, as an Oklahoma pioneer, schoolteacher, and taxpayer, she
should be qualified to vote. She was particularly incensed that at statehood she did not have a voice in the selection of constitutional delegates
who would be responsible for drafting the new state's constitution. She
protested her lack of political status by going to the polls and marking
a ballot for constitutional delegates regardless of the fact that it was not
legal to do so. When she handed her ballot to the election officials, she
remarked, "I wonder whether there will be as vigorous a protest against
me when I go to pay my taxes as when I asked for representation as a taxpayer."[30] Ultimately Cobb informed the National Woman's Party that she
was going to ask Laskey to sponsor the party's legislation.

The general attitude of Oklahoma women toward the work of the
Woman's Party in the state was negative, bordering on hostile. The opposition to the equal rights amendment encompassed several positions.
State Federation of Labor President Edgar Fenton and others who were
concerned with the needs of labor believed that an equal rights amendment would be an "abrogation of the welfare laws for women." Fenton
thought that the Federation of Labor had fought a tough battle to secure
these laws, and an equal rights amendment for women would render them
null and void.[31] The federation president was in the same camp as many
politically active women who fought for protective legislation for women

and children working in industry. Women who belonged to organizations such as the Consumers' League, Women's Trade Union League, Young Women's Christian Association, the League of Women Voters, and the United States Women's Bureau were successful in gaining legislation that offered a minimum wage and minimum working hours for women, and prohibited women from night work and certain dangerous occupations. During the Industrial Era, when most court rulings favored business, courts upheld protective legislation for women. An equal rights amendment to the federal constitution would place working-class women on an equal basis with men, many of whom did not enjoy the benefits of protective legislation. Equality meant less protection and a step backward in improving welfare for working-class women.[32]

After striking out with Edgar Fenton, Cobb took her legislation to Kathryn Van Leuven, assistant attorney general. Evidently Cobb believed that women in political positions would certainly help to advance the political equality of all women. Van Leuven, like Senator Looney, was hesitant to get involved in legislation that was seemingly so radical. Cobb concluded that Van Leuven was not a pioneer in the women's movement but a good worker who stayed behind the "firing line consolidating the gains." But what really astonished Cobb about Van Leuven's position was her view on suffrage. "She thinks women should not demand things, but only request them, and that suffrage is an experiment. Rather a conservative, I would say."[33]

When Cobb left the assistant attorney general's office, she called on a good friend of Van Leuven's, Margaret McVean, an Oklahoma City attorney. Cobb had written to McVean several times inviting her to join the NWP, but McVean did not reply to the letters. Undaunted, Cobb forged ahead looking for support for the National Woman's Party and its legislative program. During her appointment with McVean, the Oklahoma City attorney spelled out for Cobb why Oklahoma women did not support the Woman's Party. She explained that Oklahoma women resented women from the East, "foreigners," visiting the state and telling Oklahoma women how to manage the affairs of the state's women. In particular, they did not like the philosophy of New York socialite and national president of the Woman's Party Alva Belmont (inheritor of the Vanderbilt and Belmont fortunes).[34] Her views on the future of the party were, perhaps, a little too radical for politically conservative Oklahoma women. The national president believed that the power of women through the party would grow to such proportions that eventually there would be a women's dictatorship

The Age of Brass or The Triumph of Woman's Rights, Currier and Ives, 1869

where the will of the party would be imposed on the world, and all would work for peace and prosperity.[35] The party spared Oklahoma women Belmont's radical views when, in January 1923, they bypassed Belmont and sent the national secretary, Anita Pollitzer, to Oklahoma to help Cobb find support for NWP legislation and to recruit women into the party. Pollitzer targeted labor commissioner Claude Connally as a likely person to recommend NWP legislation, including an equal rights bill, to state legislators. Connally was not too interested in Pollitzer's legislation, especially if it weakened hard-fought-for protective legislation for women in industry. When Pollitzer tried to convince Connally that the word "persons" should be substituted for women in the minimum wage law, he, like the president of the Federation of Labor, stood firm against any measure that weakened the benefits of women in industry. After their disappointing meeting with Connally, Pollitzer and Cobb then met with state representative Anna Laskey. Over lunch at the state capital, Laskey agreed to sponsor all of the legislation promoted by the NWP, including the equal rights amendment. By evening of the same day, however, Laskey had changed her mind. Giving no reason, she telephoned Cobb that she "feared she would not be able to introduce our bills after all." Laskey did agree to introduce the Minimum Wage For Women Only Bill, which was sponsored by labor commissioner Connally. Perhaps true to her Socialist convictions, Laskey fell in step with the sympathies of labor by only promoting legislation that protected women in the workforce.[36] By the end of Miss Pollitzer's visit to Oklahoma City, she had a commitment from state representative J. W. Callahan to introduce four bills to the House; a bill that provided that the place of residence of a married women did not depend on her marital status, a bill that gave women the right to administer estates, a bill that allowed that husband and wife were joint heads of the household, a bill that gave illegitimate children the same rights as children born in wedlock, and a bill giving men and women equal rights. All of Callahan's bills, except H.B. 339 on equal rights, passed the House in February 1923.[37]

The ideas of women in the Woman's party were too progressive for most Oklahoma women and certainly for Oklahoma men, who held a solid majority in the state legislature. Many of these men and women held strong religious convictions based on a strict interpretation of the Bible. When Cobb heard that the Committee on Criminal Jurisprudence was going to write an unfavorable opinion on an NWP bill providing equality in the guardianship of children, Cobb met with J. D. Taylor, chairman of the committee, to understand his objections. In keeping with the age-old ideal emanating from biblical scholars and common law that in the marriage union the husband was the authority, Taylor expressed to Cobb, "The relative status of men and women was established by God, and we have no right to meddle with it." Even though Cobb offered her best argument in the matter, the committee report was negative.[38]

In March, with adjournment of the ninth legislature only weeks away, Cobb and NWP supporters lobbied for their bills to pass the Oklahoma Senate. As seen with the legislative proposals of women in the WLC and LWV, the Oklahoma legislature was not of the mind to grant women many concessions. In the final days of the session, only two bills had passed committee and made it to final readings on the floor of the Senate. The two pieces of legislation were probably the most inconsequential, but would make incremental steps toward women's equality. These bills were H.B. 340 and H.B. 338. The first would abolish the law that assumed that if a woman committed a crime in front of her husband, her husband had persuaded her to do so, and the second would grant women equality in administering estates. Cobb and other NWP lobbyists were surprised when the bills made it to the Senate floor. But at the last minute there was growing opposition from members of the Senate. Estelle Balfour, Secretary of the Oklahoma NWP, stayed on the floor of the Senate all day as she watched the bills cruise toward defeat. She later wrote, "From the first I realized there was an obstruction in our way, but did not ascertain it until yesterday. I got on the Senate floor at 9:30, and remained on the floor until 5:30, and did not leave for fear I would not get back on, and it was only by doing this that we got them advanced as far as the third reading and would have passed in to actual law today if these objections had not come up."[39]

When Florence Cobb reported to the national headquarters on the progress of NWP legislation in Oklahoma, she informed them that the "whole story is not one of defeat." The chairman of the Oklahoma NWP was happy to report that Senate Joint Resolution No. 5 would be placed on the ballot for popular vote. The resolution, which provided that women could hold state office, was offered by Oklahoma's only female state representatives, Anna Laskey, Edith Mitchell, and Lulu Anderson.[40] The fate of what became known as the "women's amendment" would be determined in a special election slated for October 2, 1923, and called by newly elected governor, "Our Man" Jack Walton. Walton called for a special election so that Oklahomans could vote on the soldiers' bonus bill and four other amendments to the state constitution. Among those amendments was Senate Joint Resolution No. 5. Politically active women hailed the special election as a good thing and believed that Oklahomans would vote favorably on the women's amendment. In fact, all indications pointed to a victory, but the political circumstances surrounding Governor Walton's first months in office brought confusion over the legitimacy of the election and demonstrated the general ineptness of politicians in interpreting Oklahoma law.

Jack Walton was an affable, handsome former Oklahoma City mayor who swept into office with the support of Socialists, Trade Unionists, and the Farmer-Labor Reconstruction League. Not long after his inauguration, Walton started to accumulate a host of enemies who resented his appointment of friends to government positions and his assault on states colleges, especially his appointment of unqualified individuals to the State Board of Regents. Walton also lost the support of the Reconstruction League, which was somewhat successful in promoting its legislative agenda to the ninth legislature despite the governor's failed promises to help. Seeing his support diminishing, Walton sought new friends. He turned to the Ku Klux Klan, a growing group of influential Oklahomans, in 1923. The Klan had opposed Walton, but they were impressed with his amicable attitude toward the order, especially after he paid a fee to become "Klansman at Large." His move to the right was only temporary. In the summer of 1923, Walton launched war on the Klan, declaring martial law in Okmulgee and Tulsa counties, and eventually extending martial law to the entire state and calling up six thousand Oklahoma guardsmen.

It was evident to many Oklahomans that Walton assumed too much power, especially after he ordered guardsmen to focus their guns on the Oklahoma County Courthouse where a grand jury was trying to meet to investigate the governor. By the end of September 1923, members of the legislature hurried back to the capital in Oklahoma City to discuss the actions of the governor. Walton barred the legislators from the capital. The lawmakers in turn met at the Skirvin Hotel in Oklahoma City, where they moved to place an initiative on the ballot of the October 2 special election. If passed by the people, the measure would amend the state constitution to authorize the legislature to call itself into special session, without the governor's invitation, in order to investigate impeachment of the governor.[41] Even though Walton tried to stop the election through his political machinations, voters turned out in record numbers to vote on Initiative No. 79, which was enthusiastically passed by more than the majority needed.[42] The original purpose of the special election, called by Walton to garner support from veterans, was evidently lost to Oklahoma voters. All five of the proposed amendments to the state constitution failed, including the women's amendment.[43]

The fate of the women's amendment took an odd turn at this juncture. The amendment did receive a majority of the votes cast (118,181 in favor and 61,577 against). But according to the state constitution, an initiative has to have a majority of the votes cast at the election plus it must be subject to a "silent vote." A silent vote is essentially a counting of all ballots cast, including those questions on the ballots that were left blank. By this procedure, a measure may pass the popular vote, but if the unmarked questions were subtracted from all ballots cast, the measure could fail by the silent vote. All five amendments, including the women's amendment, lost by the silent vote. The Oklahoma voters knew all about Governor Walton, his crusade against the Klan, and his siege of the state; but thry cared little about the other referenda on the ballot.[44] Politically active women in the state assumed that their amendment had lost and that all their efforts to gain political equality in the state were also lost.

Governor Walton's first response to the outcome of the special election was to fight the issue by declaring the election illegal. He appealed to the Supreme Court to throw out the election on the grounds that the Klan controlled the election process in the cities, so, therefore, the vote count was fraudulent.[45] The governor's fight to stop the impeachment momentum was joined by Mrs. R. L. Fite, vice chairman of the State Democrat Committee and special advisor to Walton.[46] Fite had been active politically in Oklahoma since the granting of suffrage to Oklahoma women in 1918. She was a delegate to the Democrat National Convention in San Francisco in 1920 and organized women into the Democrat party. Regardless of her efforts on behalf of Oklahoma women to gain political equality in the state, Fite was criticized savagely by Oklahoma women and newspaper editors for her association with Walton and her "selfish" political position, which many believed did not consider the greater good of all people. In her defense, Fite exclaimed that the women's amendment failed "on account of the abnormal excitement caused by the injection into the campaign at the eleventh hour, of [Initiative] No. 79. We feel that we were sacrificed. We are not pro-Walton or anti-Walton, pro-Klan or anti-Klan, or even Democrats or Republicans. We are women, standing together for what we believe to be fair play for our sex." Newspaper accounts were quick to point out that

THE DAILY OKLAHOMAN

OKLAHOMA CITY, THURSDAY, OCTOBER 11, 1920

WOMEN FIGHT VOTE RESULT

Party Leader Files Petition On Lines of Walton Plea to Kill Election

Mrs. R. L. Fite, Muskogee, vice chairman of the democratic state central committee, and a supporter of Governor Walton, filed a petition in district court Wednesday, which aligns the Woman's party in the state with the governor in his attempt to invalidate the election of October 2 by injunction proceedings.

Mrs. Fite's petition has to do with the women's rights amendment which was submitted to vote as one of the six questions.

Judge T. G. Chambers postponed the hearing on the Walton injunction until October 22 by an order Wednesday.

Uses Walton's Arguments

Entering the case as an interyenor, Mrs. Fite adopts the arguments made in Walton's petition and asks that the vote cast in Question No. 122 be not counted. She complains that no registration was hold before the election, and that sample ballots were not printed in newspapers in all the counties as directed by law.

Finally, the women's spokesman argues that the injection of Question No. 79 authorizing the legislature to meet without call by the governor, carried away all other interest in the election and caused the women's amendment to be overlooked by many voters.

Asked Finding for Majority

On this basis, Mrs. Fite asks, in case the court should throw out only the vote on the impeachment bill, that it should make a finding to the effect that the women's amendment received a majority of the votes validly cat and is adopted.

The effect of the intervention, if the election should be invalidated, would be to permit the women's amendment to be submitted again before the next regular session of the legislature.

Would Omit "Male"

The proposed amendment was to readopt the section of the constitution which states the qualification for the municipal state offices, but to omit the word male, opening the offices for women citizens as well as men. Mrs. Florence E. Cobb, of Wewoka, president of the Woman's Party in Oklahoma filed the petition for Mrs. Fite.

Daily Oklahoman Oct. 11, 1923

most women did not approve of Fite's efforts to overturn the election. The general thought was that women should sacrifice their own political equality for the good of the state, which meant getting rid of Walton.[47] Other women saw the defeat of the women's amendment as an indication that women were, after all, not interested in or suited to sharing political equality with men. Cora Miley's column in *Harlow's Weekly* fashioned a story that revealed a new conservative outlook concerning the role of the "new woman." Miley considered it foolish to fight the defeat of the women's amendment. Women, she believed, were not of the "temperament for offices of governor, corporation commissioner, attorney-general, supreme court, judge, senator, or representative." Miley pointed out that Oklahoma already had a woman senator and several women representatives. "Is there a single piece of constructive legislation from them?" she asked. Miley simply believed that women did not have the strength or endurance to fight for liberty. But they would make good clerks because of their "capacity for detail."[48]

Mrs. Fite's efforts to overturn the election were as successful as those of Walton. As it turned out, she raised the ire of women and political observers for nothing. The women's amendment passed by a majority and legally was not subject to a silent vote. Evidently the women's amendment was not the product of an initiative but a measure originating in the legislature. The state constitution allowed that an amendment originating in the legislature and presented to the people for a popular vote only needed a majority to pass. An Initiative originating from the people and placed on the ballot needed a majority plus the silent vote.[49] It is difficult to imagine that the politically astute did not understand this point in law. But once again, the victory women enjoyed over the passage of the women's amendment was short-lived. The students of political procedure also missed that it took a two-thirds majority in the House of Representatives before a measure could be submitted for a vote. For two years, women believed their amendment had passed and that they could run for state office. But in 1925, after the Oklahoma Supreme Court ruled that the school levy amendment was not eligible to be placed on the ballot at the October 2, 1923, special election, Miss Una Lee Roberts, assistant secretary of state, researched the women's amendment and found that it also was not legal because it did not receive a two-thirds majority in the house.[50] The Court voted a case before the Oklahoma Supreme Court challenging the validity of the amendment in 1930. The amendment was finally defeated, and women could not hold state office until the issue resurfaced in the early 1940s. In 1942 state citizens voted once again on the issue. This time the amendment passed without any legal disqualification.[51]

Members of the Women's Legislative Council, the League of Women Voters, and the National Woman's Party all fought for legislation to better the lives of women. Each group stressed different issues in their proposed legislation to Oklahoma lawmakers. Women who were members of the WLC believed it important to improve the health and well-being of Oklahoma women and their families. Their concerns were typical of most women in the 1920s. It was within their traditional role as mothers and homemakers to fight for reforms that benefited the family and the home. Women in the WLC also expressed, through their legislative proposals, their political philosophy concerning the role of government in providing solutions to societal problems. They believed it inefficient and a waste of legislative resources to establish new laws, whereas educating Oklahomans to the laws that were already on the books was more productive. They did see, however, that some new laws were necessary for the welfare of society. But they believed in state instead of federal legislation. The women who joined the League of Women Voters had a more progressive attitude than the women in the WLC. Members of the LWV planned legislation that would better the condition of women, especially women in industry. Unlike the WLC, the LWV was a national organization whose members advocated federal legislation over that of individual states.

The National Women's Party was certainly the most radical of women's political organizations in the 1920s. The women in the party abandoned all other issues to concentrate on a women's equal rights amendment to the federal constitution. Many women outside the party opposed such an amendment because it would negate all their hard work to secure protective legislation for women and children. Women in the NWP were at the left side of the political spectrum. They were feminists, a term with negative connotations for many in the 1920s, who believed that women should stand on an equal basis with men in all aspects of life. Many women in the 1920s disagreed with the ideological scope of the NWP. Alice Robertson of Muskogee, Oklahoma, was one of them. She was an antifeminist, antisuffrage conservative who voters in the second district elected to the United States House of Representatives in 1920. Robertson was the second woman in U.S. history elected to the U.S. Congress and epitomizes the conservatism of many Oklahoma women.

NOTES

1. Anna Korn, "The Women's Legislative Council and Its Relationship to Government," Anna Korn Collection, Oklahoma Historical Society, Oklahoma City, Oklahoma. Hereafter cited AKC.

2. J. Stanley Lemons, *The Woman Citizen Social Feminism in the 1920s*, (Urbana: University of Illinois Press, 1973), p. 55; Sophonisba P. Breckinridge, *Women in the Twentieth Century: A Study of Their Political, Social and Economic Activities*, (New York: McGraw-Hill, 1933), p. 259; Anne Firor Scott, "After Suffrage: Southern Women in the Twenties," *Journal of Southern History* 30 (August 1964): 289–318.

3. *Harlow's Weekly*, 29 October 1920; Korn, "Women's Legislative Council and Its Relationship to Government," AKC.

4. Korn was also an artist and a musician. Many of her original musical compositions received national recognition. Her song, "Guard the Flag of Our Republic," was sung by the Washington Memorial Choir at the dedication of Patriots' Hall at Valley Forge, Virginia. Also, one of her pastel paintings won first prize in an art exhibition at the Oklahoma State Fair. *Harlow's Weekly*, 30 July 1920; Rex Harlow, *Makers of Government in Oklahoma* (Oklahoma City: Harlow's Publishing Company, 1930) p. 63. On the association of the Masons with the Ku Klux Klan see Angie Debo, *Prairie City*, (Tulsa: Council Oak Books, LTD, 1985), p. 166.

5. *Harlow's Weekly*, 17 December 1920.

6. *Harlow's Weekly*, 29 October 1920, 17 December 1920, 24 December 1920.

7. *Harlow's Weekly*, 12 December 1920.

8. Anna Korn, "Women's Legislative Council and Its Relationship to Government," AKC.

9. *Harlow's Weekly*, 15 April 1921.

10. Ibid.

11. *Harlow's Weekly*, 15 December 1921.

12. Ibid.; Directory of Oklahoma, 1989–1990 State Almanac (Oklahoma City: Oklahoma Publishing Company).

13. Lemons, *The Woman Citizen*, p. 181.

14. Seth Koven and Sonya Michel, editors, *Mothers of a New World, Maternalist Politics and the Origins of Welfare States*, (New York: Routledge, 1993), pp. 4–11.

15. In 1890 the National Woman Suffrage Association joined the American Woman Suffrage Association to form the National American Woman Suffrage Association (NAWSA). The new organization adopted a conservative approach in winning suffrage by concentrating the fight in the states where new suffrage organizations pressured legislators to amend state constitutions

to allow women to vote. Ida Husted Harper, *History of Woman Suffrage*, Vol. 6, 1900–1920, (New York: Arno, 1969), p. 685.

16. *Harlow's Weekly*, 25 June 1920, 27 August 1920, 12 November 1920, 10 December 1920, 17 December 1920, 24 December 1920.

17. *Harlow's Weekly*, 14 January 1921.

18. *Harlow's Weekly*, 1 July 1921.

19. Assigning the label of feminist to politically active women began around 1910. According to Nancy Cott in *The Grounding of Modern Feminism*, the principles of feminism replaced the ideals incorporated into the woman movement of the nineteenth century, principally the issues of women's rights, suffrage, and welfare. In the twentieth century, feminism took on a different connotation, signifying a more radical point of view concerning the relations between the sexes. Cott's construction of feminism informs that women's inequality was socially fashioned; therefore, it could be changed. And women's condition was shared experience—women needed to work together to bring about change that benefited the welfare of all women. Nancy F. Cott, *Grounding of Modern Feminism*, (New Haven: Yale University Press, 1987), pp. 4–5.

20. Mary Anne Baker, Catherine White Berheide, Fay Ross Greckel, Linda Carstarphen Gugin, Marcia J. Lipetz, Marcia Texler Segal, *Women Today: A Multidisciplinary Approach to Women's Studies*, (Monterey: Brooks/Cole Publishing Company, 1980), chapter one; Cott, *Grounding of Modern Feminism*, chapter two.

21. *Harlow's Weekly*, 13 August 1920.

22. Emma Estill Harbour was head of the History Department and professor of history and social science at Central State University in Edmond, Oklahoma. She was born in Liberty, Missouri, in 1884. She relocated to Oklahoma in 1907. She was a graduate of Colorado College in Colorado Springs, and of Oklahoma College for Women. She received her M.A. and Ph.D. from the University of Oklahoma. Along with being active in Democrat politics, she was associated with various conservative organizations: Daughters of the American Revolution, Daughters of the American Colonists, and the American legion. Harlow, *Makers of Government in Oklahoma*, p. 511.

23. *Harlow's Weekly*, 19 November 1920, 18 February 1921.

24. Cott, *Grounding of Modern Feminism*, pp. 67–72.

25. *Harlow's Weekly*, 18 March 1921.

26. National Woman's Party to Florence Cobb, 11 October 1922, National Woman's Party Collection, microfilm, Bizzell Library, University of Oklahoma, Norman, Oklahoma. Hereafter cited NWPC. Florence Cobb led a distinguished professional career in Oklahoma. Before moving to Oklahoma she was employed in the Census Bureau, Department of Commerce, and

in the office of Indian Affairs. In Oklahoma, while working as Librarian in Charge of the City Library of Wewoka, she served two terms of office as Justice of the Peace. In 1933 she was appointed Municipal Judge of the City of Wewoka and was active in civic and church affairs of that city. She died in 1946. "Necrology" *Chronicles of Oklahoma* 24 (1947); Lyle H. Boren and Dale Boren, *Who Is Who In Oklahoma*, (Guthrie: Co-Operative Publishing Company, 1935), p. 99.

27. *Harlow's Weekly*, 18 March 1920.
28. *Harlow's Weekly*, 14 January 1921, 28 January 1921.
29. Florence Cobb to National Woman's Party, 6 January 1922, NWPC.
30. *Daily Oklahoman*, 23 November 1906; Harlow, *Makers of Government in Oklahoma*, p. 541.
31. Florence Cobb to Alice Paul, 23 November 1922, NWPC.
32. Lemons, *Woman Citizen*, p. 146.
33. Florence Cobb to Alice Paul, 23 November 1922, NWPC.
34. Ibid; Cott, *Grounding of Modern Feminism*, pp. 33, 55.
35. Lemons, *Woman Citizen*, p. 109.
36. Florence Cobb to National Woman's Party, 17 February 1923, NWPC.
37. Callahan introduced H.B. Nos. 337, 338, 340, 341, 243, and 339, "The National Woman's Party and Its Legislative Work in Oklahoma," NWPC. Information on these bills is in Oklahoma House Journal, Regular Session, Ninth Legislature, 1923; Florence Cobb to Anita Pollitzer, 13 March 1923, NWPC.
38. Florence Cobb to National Woman's Party, 17 February 1923, NWPC.
39. Florence Cobb to National Woman's Party, 2 April 1923, NWPC.
40. Ibid; Oklahoma, House Journal, Regular Session, Ninth Legislature, 1923.
41. Danny Goble, *Oklahoma Politics: A History*, (University of Oklahoma Press, 1982), pp. 118–124; *Harlow's Weekly*, 6 October 1923.
42. The final tally was 188,573 yes, 57,899 no. *Harlow's Weekly*, 6 October 1923.
43. The five amendments were the Soldiers' Bonus, School Levy, Workmen's Compensation, Bank Refund, and Women's Rights. *Daily Oklahoman*, 3 October 1923.
44. David R. Morgan, Robert E. England, and George G. Humphreys, *Oklahoma Politics and Policies: Governing the Sooner State*, (Lincoln: University of Nebraska Press, 1991), p. 69.
45. *Daily Oklahoman*, 4 October 1923.
46. *Harlow's Weekly*, 7 July 1922.
47. *Harlow's Weekly*, 10 October 1923.
48. *Harlow's Weekly*, 3 November 1923.

49. Morgan, England, Humphreys, *Oklahoma Politics and Policies: Governing the Sooner State*, p.70.
50. *Harlow's Weekly*, 12 September 1925.
51. The Oklahoma Supreme Court ruled that the October 1923 special election was invalid. See *Looney v. Leeper*, 145 Okla. 202,292 P 365 (1930). Janice P. Dreiling, "Women and Oklahoma Law: How It Has Changed, Who Changed It, and What Is Left," *Oklahoma Law Review* (1997): 417.

A Political Conservative: Alice Robertson, United States Congresswoman from Oklahoma

In the want-ad section of the *Muskogee Daily Phoenix*, Alice Robertson advertised for customers to visit her cafeteria in downtown Muskogee, while at the same time using the ad to campaign for a seat in the United States Congress. Because the daily newspapers little recognized her candidacy, Robertson had to resort to paid advertisements to inform Oklahomans of her political capabilities. Her column-length ad entitled "Sawokla Cafeteria" provided a down-to-earth, Will Rogers–type folksiness that made her a popular and successful congressional candidate in 1920. But surprisingly, in the year that women worked together to fight for political equality, Robertson's support was mostly from ex-servicemen whom she befriended through her work with the Red Cross during the first World War. And ironically, just as the servicemen helped to elect her to Congress, they turned against her when she did not support the Soldiers' Bonus Bill, ultimately working toward her congressional defeat in November 1922. The appearance of not understanding the concerns of her constituents made the sixty-six-year-old congresswoman seem politically inept. But Robertson was a strong-willed individual who one political commentator characterized as feminine, yet having "a very masculine ability."[1] The commentator was correct in his assessment. Robertson was a very politically astute woman for her time who knew that professional opportunities were found by making friends in political circles. She approached her career opportunities with a very "masculine ability," never stopping to think that the offices to which she aspired might be outside the possibilities of her gender. Robertson also developed a political philosophy that guided her down unpopular paths that many a seasoned politician would never travel. This was especially true in her short tenure as congresswoman. During her congressional years, Robertson was confronted with many difficult legislative decisions. She typically voted according

THE DAILY OKLAHOMAN

OKLAHOMA CITY, FRIDAY, NOVEMBEr 5, 1920

WOMAN WINNER ON 'WANT' ADS

Voters Declare She Forced Way to Their Hearts by Stomach Rout.

(By Associated Press State Wire.)

MUSKOGEE, Okla. Nov. 4, Little "want ads" appearing in daily papers carried such an appeal to the voters of the second Oklahoma congressional district that they elected Miss Alice M. Robertson to congress. This was what the second woman to hold a congressional seat in American political history had to say about her victory today. She is 65 years old and admits it quite willingly.

The voters, however, declare Miss Robertson won her way to their ballots "through their stomachs." They declare the meals she served in her little restaurant here were such as to swing "mere man" to her support without further ado. Political leaders declare woman suffrage gave Miss Robertson her victory.

Miss Robertson goes to congress with a long record of public achievement in Muskogee and the surrounding countryside. She has always been an ardent exponent of legislation favoring the Indians and declared today she would specialize on favorable Indian laws during her service in congress. She was born in Indian Territory and her previous public service has been characterized by deeds in behalf of Oklahoma's Indian population.

She held public office once before during President Roosevelt's second term where he appointed her postmistress of Muskogee. She has long been identified with public charities heading the entire Red Cross organization of Muskogee county during the war.

Daily Oklahoman, Nov. 5, 1920

to her strong belief in conservative fiscal and social policies, which she perceived were good for the people she represented in Oklahoma's second district and for the greater good of the nation.

Alice Robertson's candidacy for the United States Congress did not come as a surprise to many who considered her the most capable woman to aspire to such a high political office. She was well known in eastern Oklahoma for her missionary work among the Creek Nation and as the decedent of prominent missionaries who worked among the Five Tribes in Indian Territory. Robertson was the granddaughter of missionary Dr. Samuel A. Worcester, whose family accompanied the forced removal of the Cherokees from Georgia to Indian Territory in 1835.[2] Worcester's daughter, Ann Eliza Worcester, and her husband, Rev. William Schenk Robertson, were also well known Presbyterian missionaries. Ann Eliza worked with her husband at Tullahassee Mission, where she mastered the Creek language and ultimately translated the New Testament into Creek. She later received an honorary doctor of philosophy degree for her work. On January 2, 1854, Ann Eliza took a leave of absence from her teaching responsibilities at Tullahassee to give birth to Alice Mary Robertson. The young "Miss Alice" grew up understanding the missionary principles and the philanthropic impulse of her family—she spent most of her life serving others. Her involvement in politics was an extension of her missionary life.[3]

Robertson's education, work experiences, and political friendships in early life helped to shape the direction of her political career. In 1871, at the age of seventeen, she left Indian Territory to attend Elmira College in Elmira, New York. At Elmira, she studied history, English, and civics. An extension of her civics course was periodic trips to Washington, D.C., where she met different political personalities, including President and Mrs. Grant and various congressmen introduced to her by her old acquaintance Pleasant Porter, chief of the Creek Nation. Political connections that her family made through their missionary work in Indian Territory helped Robertson to obtain her first government position. Senator O. H. Platt of Connecticut, chairman of the Committee on Indian Affairs, was a great admirer of Robertson's family and helped her to secure a job with the federal Indian Department in Washington, D.C., in 1873. Robertson was the first woman clerk to work in the Indian office. While in Washington, she furthered her education by taking courses in shorthand and domestic science, and continued to make the acquaintance of those who were prominent in the political and social life of the nation's capital. She attended numerous political functions, including a reception in honor of Mrs. Ulysses S. Grant, Mrs. Rutherford B. Hayes, and Mr. and Mrs. James A. Garfield.[4]

In 1878 Alice returned to Tullahassee Mission to help her mother with mission responsibilities. The Indian Department in Washington continued to pay her salary, and in 1880 the department transferred her to Carlisle Indian School in Pennsylvania as secretary to superintendent, Captain R. H. Pratt.[5] Even though Robertson worked in the East, she never lost interest in the education and well-being of Native American children in Indian Territory. When fire destroyed much of Tullahassee Mission in 1880, Robertson took a leave of absence from Carlisle to lobby Indian office administrators to make arrangements at Carlisle for twenty-five students from the mission. She even secured train passage for the students by soliciting donations from her wealthy cousin E. D. Worcester and the Russell Sage Foundation. Robertson eventually returned to Indian Territory in 1882 to accept a teaching position at the Creek School in Okmulgee. Ultimately, she was instrumental in securing funding for Nuyaka Mission School, where her sister Ann Augusta became superintendent, and in 1885 Robertson took charge of raising funds for Minerva Home, a boarding school for girls, which later became Henry Kendall College, today's University of Tulsa.[6]

Alice's work and experience in Indian Territory provided her with the expertise needed to become involved in the Indian Reform Movement in the late nineteenth century. It was through this avenue that she continued to meet influential people who eventually helped her political career. Especially beneficial was her attendance at the annual conference on Indian reform held by the Quaker organization, "Friends of the Indians" at Lake Mohonk, near New Paltz, New York. The Lake Mohonk Conference began in 1883 on the property of Quaker schoolteacher Albert K. Smiley, a member of the Board of Indian Commissioners. The purpose was to provide board members and other interested individuals a meeting place where they could casually discuss Indian affairs. In subsequent years, the conference grew to include various seminars where a variety of experts delivered speeches concerning some aspect of Indian reform. In 1892 conference organizers asked Alice Robertson to speak of her missionary work with the Five Civilized Tribes in Indian Territory. Among those listening to her speech was Theodore Roosevelt, civil service commissioner in President Benjamin Harrison's administration.[7] The subsequent meeting between Alice Robertson and Theodore Roosevelt was the beginning of a friendship that lasted until Roosevelt's death in 1919.

The speech that Robertson delivered at the conference revealed her brand of political conservatism, from which she never wavered throughout her professional life. When she first started attending the Lake Mohonk Conference in 1889, she held more conservative views than most of her contemporaries; she did not believe that Indian people were ready to assume private ownership of their lands as recommended by Indian reformers. Over time, however, she saw that the present system of communal ownership was not advantageous to the overall well-being of Indian people. In Indian Territory, she was disheartened by the corrupt practices of whites who intermarried in the tribes and of people of mixed blood; she accused both groups of swindling the people out of valuable land and natural resources. Robertson's solution to the problem was "complete jurisdiction for the United States courts in Indian Territory, allotment of lands, United States citizenship, and, as quickly as possible, statehood."[8] Robertson advocated complete independence for Indian people, which meant discontinuing the federal government's paternalistic oversight of Native American life. She based her opinion on her conviction that the country benefited from the hard work of its people, which in turn enhanced the individual's self-esteem and personal worth. Government intervention, as well intended as it might be, would undermine the accomplishments of hard work. Roosevelt agreed with Robertson and listened attentively as she applied her philosophy to the debate concerning the merits and disadvantages associated with both government and mission schools. To some at the conference, the ideal educational plan was to take young Indian children out of the mission school and place them in the government boarding school. The students would eventually return to the mission school, where they could pursue higher education. Robertson argued that it should be the other way around. She explained that the early years were the most important in which to give practical Christian training. It was also her point of view that it was easier to raise funds for the care of younger children than to find financial donors for the schooling of older children. In a similar vein, Robertson advised her audience that it was not the responsibility of government to provide an education for all students, but only for those who "show strong purpose and ability." Indian students who believed that they were qualified should apply for scholarships based on their ability. The thought was that when successful candidates finished their education, they would move back home and continue to work toward improving their own lives and the lives of those in their community. Robertson warned that if the government provided for all of the needs of the Indian youth, it would encourage a belief that "the government owes them a living."[9] Theodore Roosevelt may not have held as conservative a point of view as Robertson, but the lady missionary made an impression and perhaps helped to shape Roosevelt's ideas on Native American reform.[10] At any rate, after Robertson's speech, the young civil service commissioner approached her explaining that he "could not wait for a formal introduction. I just had to tell you how fine I thought your talk was. Your views on Indian education are mine also."[11]

The two reformers had more in common than their concern for the welfare of Native American people. They both were politically ambitious and sought opportunities to advance their careers. In 1895, New York City Mayor William L. Strong appointed Theodore Roosevelt to the position of city police commissioner. He held the position for two years until he accepted President William McKinley's appointment to assistant secretary of the navy. He supported the position of a war with Spain, and when war finally began in 1898, he volunteered, along with twenty-three thousand other men, to help defeat Spain in Cuba. He entered the Volunteer Corps as a lieutenant colonel but moved into the position of colonel when Colonel Leonard Wood was promoted to brigadier general. The men under Roosevelt's command became known as the Rough Riders and their main responsibility was to defeat the Spanish who were defending the city of Santiago de Cuba.[12] Alice Robertson sealed her relationship with Roosevelt when she helped to recruit volunteers for the Rough Riders. Most of the men in L and M troops were from Indian Territory, many of whom were Robertson's students.[13]

Roosevelt came home from Cuba a war hero and immediately turned his new popularity to his advantage; he ran for governor of New York in 1898. With his Rough Riders by his side, he launched a winning campaign, but only occupied the office for two years. While he was governor, Alice Robertson waged her own campaign to secure an appointment to the Department of the Interior as superintendent of schools in Indian Territory. She wrote to President McKinley but received no reply. Perhaps thinking that her presence in Washington would enable her to work toward the superintendent's position, she took a leave of absence from her teaching responsibilities at Henry Kendall College, and accepted a job at the U.S. Census Bureau. While in Washington, she petitioned Pleasant Porter; Dr. Merrill Gates, Secretary to the Commissioner of Indian Affairs;

her cousin D. C. Worcester, U.S. Commissioner to the Philippines; and finally her good friend the governor of New York, Theodore Roosevelt about the job.[14] Her accumulated good will with Roosevelt surrendered her dividends. The governor wrote to her that "few things have given me more pleasure than to write as strongly as I know how to urge your appointment as Supervisor."[15] He then wrote to the secretary of Interior, informing the secretary that he knew Alice Robertson well and that "some of her pupils were in my regiment in Cuba.... Miss Robertson has done remarkably good work and I cannot speak too highly of her."[16]

Robertson assumed her duties as superintendent of Creek schools in June of 1900. Her responsibilities included appointment of teachers, visiting schools, auditing accounts, preparing statistics, and making quarterly and annual reports. The arduous travel schedule around Indian Territory and the care of her ailing mother led her to look for other means of employment in 1904.[17] She once again appealed to her good friend Theodore Roosevelt. In 1900 President William McKinley chose Roosevelt as his vice-presidential running mate. Although many viewed the exuberant Roosevelt as anything but presidential, his place on the ticket helped the Republican party to win the presidency. And with the assassination of McKinley in 1901, Roosevelt climbed to the very top of the political ladder.[18] Alice Robertson wrote to her good friend in the White House asking him to appoint her as postmistress of the post office in Muskogee, Indian Territory. Post office appointments were traditionally a source of reward or patronage for those who supported the U.S. presidents.[19] When Roosevelt assumed the office in 1901, his first concern was to appoint key supporters to government positions, especially in the South, where the Republican party needed to bolster delegate votes for the upcoming 1904 Republican convention. The Republican party in Indian Territory expected that Roosevelt would reward a party stalwart with the "plum" of patronage positions, not a woman who they perceived to have little political clout. But Roosevelt abandoned practical political consideration and insisted that the appointment be given to Alice Robertson. He sent her nomination to the Senate in December of 1904. The Senate confirmed Robertson with little debate.

The one area in which Robertson disagreed with Roosevelt was whether Oklahoma and Indian Territory should be admitted to the Union as a single state or as two separate states. Roosevelt believed that the Twin Territories should be joined into one state called Oklahoma. Robertson thought otherwise. Her stand on the statehood issue exposed her distrust and animus toward Southern Democrats, sentiments she inherited from her grandfather's family, who had distrusted Democrats ever since President Andrew Jackson refused to uphold the Supreme Court decision of *Worcester v. Georgia*. Since the family considered Jackson the founder of the Democrat party, all Democrats were suspected of dishonesty and treachery. In Robertson's opinion, the influx of white Southerners, mostly Democrat, into Indian and Oklahoma Territories brought the worst kind of corruption and crime, especially the breed she called "Oklahomans." It was the Oklahomans who would build saloons and generally find ways in which to take advantage of the innocence of the Indian people.[20] Her views on statehood further revealed her conservative nature and staunch Republican convictions, even if it meant disagreement with Theodore Roosevelt. She wrote him many letters on the matter but to no avail.

Alice Robertson's tenure as postmaster lasted until the election of Democrat Woodrow Wilson to the presidency in 1912. During her employment in the Muskogee Post Office, she was able to save enough money to build her own home west of town on Agency Hill. Robertson's fifty-five-acre farm was the culmination of years of work to better her life. At her farm she raised vegetables, Guernsey and Jersey dairy cows, Duroc-Jersey pigs, and leghorn hens. She expanded her truck farm operation to Muskogee when she opened a cafeteria to provide an outlet for her farm products and a place where working girls could find good, wholesome, homegrown food. Her restaurant also offered women a reading room and showers. She eventually expanded her clientele to include the general public.[21]

If Robertson was not already well known in Muskogee because of her family or her political connections, she became even more popular for her kindness and charity to World War I troops as they headed through Muskogee on their way to destinations in the United States and Europe. When troop trains stopped in town, Robertson was waiting on the depot platform with surplus food from her cafeteria: doughnuts, sandwiches, and coffee. Her handouts were so warmly welcomed by the service-men that railroad personnel helped the restaurateur to establish a Red Cross Canteen in an abandoned railroad car. If soldiers had a layover in Muskogee, she invited them to her cafeteria for a free meal, and often-times she invited them to stay overnight at her farm, which she appropriately named Sawokla, a Creek word for gathering place.[22]

Alice Robertson wore many hats. She was a professional bureau-crat, a missionary, a farmer, an entrepreneur, a philanthropist, and a politician. This last profession was perhaps the most out of character for her because she did not believe in women's political equality. Robertson held such a strong conviction that women should not be given suffrage that she joined the National Association Opposed to Woman Suffrage and accepted the position of vice-president of the Oklahoma chapter. Like many women in the early twentieth century, Alice believed that politics was no place for a lady. The origins of antisuffrage sentiment can be traced back to New England, when in 1868 two hundred women protested a woman suffrage petition brought before the Massachusetts legislature. The trend to oppose suffrage grew throughout the nineteenth and early twentieth centuries. Women opposed to suffrage maintained that their place was in the home, where they had moral influence. Engaging in the business of politics was a "dirty" endeavor and would diminish women's established sphere in the home, where they upheld the virtues of American society.[23] Alice did not fit into the "woman in the home" scenario that seemed to justify antisuffrage rhetoric. She did not marry, she did not have a family, and she did not maintain a "sphere of influence" in the home. On the surface, her antisuffrage stand would seem an anomaly to the reality of her life. It was not uncommon, however, to find politically influential women taking a stand against suffrage. The president of the Oklahoma Anti-suffrage Organization, Mrs. Thomas H. Sturgeon (Sallie Lewis Stephens) established a career in journalism in Oklahoma, where she was the first to write about the concerns of women for daily newspapers and published her own weekly, *The Oklahoma Lady*. In 1920 Governor J. B. A. Robertson appointed Sturgeon to the Oklahoma State Board of Health as an inspector of public facilities. She was the first woman in the United States to serve on such a board. Regardless of her work experience outside the home, she still fought to deny women the right to vote.[24] As already mentioned, Kate Barnard, the first to hold the office of Oklahoma Commissioner of Charities and Corrections would not help suffragists in the state because it took away from her "life's work," which she considered more important than whether Oklahoma women secured political equality. Nationally renowned women like Ida Tarbell, who wrote the exposé on John Rockefeller and Standard Oil, and lesser-known but politically powerful women like Elizabeth Lowell Putnam of Massachusetts were antisuffrage advocates. These women and many like them did not believe that suffrage would add anything to women's experience. If anything, they believed that suffrage would weaken the power they already enjoyed.

Another salient reason Robertson and other antisuffrage women worked to defeat woman suffrage in Oklahoma was that they did not trust women to vote for the good of the country. The Socialists were the first political party to endorse suffrage, which attracted many women to the Socialist cause. It was also becoming more evident by voting patterns across the country that in areas where women had suffrage, Socialists gained seats in state offices and legislatures. Antisuffrage women also pointed out that the leaders of the suffrage movement "have long been identified with the Socialist and Pacifist movement."[25] The antisuffrage indictment of socialism most likely affected Robertson's political stand on the franchise. As a conservative and a patriot, Robertson believed in protecting America's cherished institutions.

Like other women who took a leading role in society, Robertson attributed the successes in her life to her own initiative, and not to her political equality. She proved this time and again, but most essentially when she decided to run for the United States Congress, only the second woman to do so in the nation's history. Suffrage did not help Robertson to climb to this high goal. Her political connections and well-known charitable deeds accounted for her success. It is not clear why Robertson chose to run for the United States House of Representatives instead of the Oklahoma house. It is known that the Oklahoma Republican party urged Robertson to run for the federal office. It can be assumed that the party believed her popularity among the people of the second district and her political connections outside the state made her an attractive candidate in 1920.[26] When she won the August 3 primary, no one was more surprised than Robertson, even though her opponents did not put up a very good fight.[27] In the November election, she faced a more formidable candidate in William Wirt Hastings of Talequah, third-term congressman from the second district. Robertson's campaign was unconventional, but ultimately successful. Instead of making campaign speeches and traveling throughout her district, she talked to residents in Oklahoma's second district through a series of ads in the *Muskogee Daily Phoenix*. Her want-ad column informed voters about her views on what she planned to do for folks in her district and related a home spun philosophy about the work that citizens could do for the good of all society. In several of her columns, she discussed the need for veterans' hospital in Oklahoma. Her concern for the soldiers who sacrificed so much for the good of the country seemed to permeate much of her life. She took it as her personal obligation to insure the comfort and well-being of those who sacrificed so

Men looking in window of National Anti-Suffrage Association, 1911

much. She promised that she would fight in Congress for a veterans' hospital in Oklahoma so that war veterans of the state would not have to go as far as Houston to receive medical attention. In her column, Robertson also asked citizens to take the time to recognize the valiant soldiers. In a sermonette-type discourse, Robertson admonished Oklahomans to follow God's example by taking care of those who were in need of a gentle word or a giving hand. She related that "The infinite mind of God keeps each one in remembrance and not one is lost or forgotten. It is only we self absorbed humans who forget." But she made it clear that she was not asking for anything more than a caring hand. She was "not suggesting alms for those who saved our country."[28] This was a stand that she would continue to take throughout her short political life. Besides her column in the want ads of the *Muskogee Daily Phoenix*, Robertson used her home to entertain voters of the second district. At one barbecue, a plane circled overhead with a banner that read, "Vote for Miss Alice." Robertson won the congressional seat in the United States House of Representative by a very narrow margin. When all votes were counted, she held the lead by 209 votes.

Robertson was very excited about being the second woman in U.S. history to be elected to the United States Congress. She wrote to friends that "It is like a dream isn't it?" She also elaborated on her intentions as a congresswoman. First she advised people to call her "congressman" or "representative from the second district of Oklahoma," but not to call her "congresswoman." She explained that she would pattern her congressional style after that of the men, accepting only those social obligations befitting male members of Congress. She would not attend "pink teas" or afternoon receptions. When she was not busy attending to the business of the House, she would work on her book. Robertson evidently had been working on a book for some time and believed now that she was a member of Congress, she would be able to find a publisher. Her book was so important to her that she planned to live in a hotel close to libraries and Congress so that she could do research.[29] After she arrived in Washington, the congresswoman used her political connections to secure committee appointments where she believed she had the most expertise. She asked her mother's cousin's husband, Senator Fred Hale to use his connections to help her obtain a position on the Committee on Indian Affairs. She also was appointed to the Committee on Expenditures in the Department of the Interior. And ironically, the antisuffrage congresswoman was chosen to be a member of the House Suffrage Committee.[30]

The congresswoman associated with the most politically conservative members of Congress. She also made conservative friends outside of government, who used their financial influence to maintain the moral and religious character of American life.[31] Mary Thaw, the wife of William Thaw who made a fortune in the railroad and coke industries in Pittsburgh, Pennsylvania, was one of Alice's benefactors. Robertson's acquaintance with Thaw went back to missionary days in Indian Territory. Thaw was associated with the Presbyterian Board of Home Mission, the missionary board that sponsored Alice's parents' missionary work. Thaw encouraged Alice's mother's work translating the Bible into the Creek language and provided necessary funding to make the project possible. Thaw customarily offered financial assistance to further the spread of Christianity and to uphold Christian values in the United States.[32] She became one of Alice Robertson's political supporters and often lent Robertson necessary funds to expand her "homespun" wardrobe so that the congresswoman could make a good appearance when assuming her professional and social duties.

Although Mary Thaw was generous with her financial assistance to Alice, mostly through noninterest loans, the wealthy benefactor did not influence Robertson's stand on key issues. Thaw would often send the congresswoman articles pointing out a particular point of view and debating the merits of the issue. But there is no evidence that Thaw influenced Robertson's decisions concerning House legislation. In fact, Robertson stood her ground on certain issues that she believed very important to the nation, in particular, her stand against the League of Nations. Thaw was a supporter of Woodrow Wilson and believed in his vision for a new world order as embraced in the League of Nations. Wilson's missionary diplomacy and religious background was a pertinent factor in Thaw's support of his policies. In contrast, Thaw disliked President Harding and considered him antireligious and rude to foreign dignitaries when they visited the United States. Evidently, it was Harding's policy to allow visiting heads of state to pay for their own food and lodging. Thaw believed that Robertson could have some kind of influence over the lack of religious fervor in the Harding administration. She asked Robertson as "a Republican, an American, and a Christian" to talk to Harding about his lack of religiosity. Unlike Thaw, Robertson did not support the League of Nations and had a completely different view of the Harding administration than her benefactor. In fact, on most issues, she followed Harding's lead and voted the party line.[33]

THE DAILY OKLAHOMAN

OKLAHOMA CITY, SUNDAY, JUNE 5, 1921

Oklahoma's Own Alice Is Making Good in House

Fails At Pie Distribution But She's Got Conviction And Fights for Them; Asks "Miss" Be Dropped.

By Staff Correspondent.

WASHINGTON, JUNE 4—Miss Alice Robertson Congresswoman from Oklahoma, and the second woman to occupy a seat in the United States house of representatives, is making good.

This is the unanimous opinion of her colleagues on the floor of the house, of newspaper men in the gallery whose opinions are not to be disregarded and of civic and social organizations in Washington where the Oklahoma woman is in great demand as a speaker.

Woman's Party Supplies Critics

Strange as it may seem, the only criticism of "Miss Alice" comes from the National Woman's Party and those women who are classed as militant suffragists.

They are openly unfriendly to the only one of their sex who occupies a seat in the National Congress and Miss Alice, with that independence that characterized her New England ancestry, welcomes their enmity.

As a matter of fact, she already has thrown down the gauntlet to them and, at every opportunity during her numerous speeches before various organizations in the east, she issues a new deft.

Approach Task Trembling.

But, to get back to the question of making good, Miss Alice has occupied her sear in the house for nearly three months. She approached the day when she was to take that seat with trembling and apprehension. She would not feel "at home" as one woman among "so many" men, she said.

The day finally arrived and she steeled herself for the ordeal. She found the "men folk" extremely kind and courteous and it was only a few days before Miss Alice felt her natural independence returning to her and was insisting that the kindness and courtesy should not reach a degree where cognizance should be take of the fact that she was a woman.

Daily Oklahoman, June 5, 1921

The congresswoman's reputation for honesty and for voting her conscience was evident in the stand she took on two controversial pieces of legislation presented to the House during her term in Congress. The first was the passage of a protective tariff. In June 1922 Robertson addressed members of the House concerning her views on the necessity of a protective tariff. As she often did, she began her speech with a colorful description of her early life in Indian Territory, but as always, her introduction was pertinent to the subject at hand. She informed the members that while working as a teacher to Indian girls in Muskogee in 1889, she was asked to act as a stenographer for the Cherokee Commission which was in Indian Territory negotiating a treaty with the Cherokee Nation for cession of its lands. While sitting around the campfire one night, the chairman of the commission, David H. Jerome, former governor of Michigan who had been consul general and minister in England, France, and Spain, explained his views on protective tariffs. The commissioner related that during the Civil War a protective tariff had benefited the North and ultimately helped in the northern victory. The South, on the other hand, was handicapped by free trade principles. The chairman maintained that America's freedom and prosperity lay in trade protectionist policies. Robertson's education at the hands of the chairman of the Cherokee Commission stood her well as a civics teacher and as a member of the House of Representatives. Her argument to the House was that supporting a protective tariff was supporting patriotism. A revenue tariff and a tax on commodities not produced in the United States, as championed by some, would not raise as much revenue as would a protective tariff. Robertson used the Oklahoma farmer as an example of how free trade policies hurt the livelihood of many people. She explained how well Oklahoma farmers were doing until after World War I, when Wilson initiated free-trade programs. The bottom fell out of the agriculture market, causing undue suffering to farmers. Only under the protective tariff were they able to compete fairly in the marketplace.[34]

Even though Robertson supported the idea of a protective tariff, she was offended by the regional bias of congressmen. A heated debate ensued over the placing of oil on the tariff list. Of course, it was the belief of those members from oil-producing states that oil should be included so as to protect the oil production in their region, but this was not the sentiment of a majority of the membership, and ultimately, oil was not included in the tariff. What incensed the congresswoman was the argument of New England legislators who insisted that hides be included on the tariff list so as to protect the shoe industry in New England. She broke from the party line and did not support adding hides to the list.[35] In her discussion about the tariff, Robertson also drew a connection between women's responsibilities in the home and the value of a protective tariff. Her view was that free trade robbed Americans of jobs because foreign goods would flood into the country at a noncompetitive price, thereby eliminating manufacturing of American goods. When husbands, brothers, and fathers were without jobs, women could not do their duty in the home. American youth would also suffer under free-trade policies. There would be little reason to acquire an education to seek employment in American business or industry, if these industries were idle because of foreign competition.[36] Her notoriety for speaking her mind and voting against the will of the party on this issue inspired Oklahoma women to form their own tariff clubs to educate one another about such political subjects that were generally not in women's sphere of interest.[37]

Robertson was outspoken on the tariff issue, but not as vociferous as she was on the Adjusted Compensation or Soldiers' Bonus Bill. The Soldiers' Bonus Bill was one of the campaign promises made by Republicans in their bid for support in the 1920 election. Veterans' groups who believed that they should be compensated for their economic loss while serving their country initiated the bill. Robertson, although the most ardent supporter of soldiers and veterans of foreign wars, took the unpopular position that government should not compensate men for serving their country. In her campaign, Alice pledged to support relief measures for veterans. Principally, she supported and worked actively to help pass legislation in Oklahoma for veterans' hospitals. In March of 1921, the Oklahoma legislature passed a law deeding forty acres to the federal government for the hospital. If the state and the federal government could not come to an agreement, then the state would appropriate $100,000 for a future hospital in the state. Ultimately, the state built the veterans' hospital in Muskogee and asked Robertson to negotiate an agreement with the federal government wherein the state would lease the veterans' facility to them.[38]

Robertson did not view the Soldiers' Bonus Bill in the same light as providing federal aid through a veterans' hospital. Her opposition to the Bonus Bill evolved from two things: her perception of the economic situation in the country in 1921, and her ideals concerning patriotism. It was her contention that when President Harding assumed his office, he inherited an economic mess from Woodrow Wilson's administration. Even though the Republicans supported compensation for soldiers, President Harding withdrew his endorsement, maintaining that the government could not afford the drain on its financial resources. Hearing that the country could not afford such a financial burden struck a chord with Robertson; she followed the president's lead by voting against the measure.[39] It is unlikely that many Americans knew or cared how the congresswoman from Oklahoma voted on compensation for World War I veterans. It would have gone unnoticed if she had not given a speech on the subject to the Woman's Republican Club in New York City in February of 1922. As the second woman to occupy a seat in Congress, Robertson's speeches tended to be covered by some of the country's larger newspapers. The coverage of her speech to the Republican ladies circulated throughout the country and cast an unfavorable light on her position concerning the Bonus Bill. Basically she was trying to explain that there was no precedent set for extra financial remuneration for those who served in war. She pointed to her own ancestors and all others who fought in the Civil War and the Spanish American War who did not ask for a bonus for their service. Her speech ended with an unfortunate comment, "If the veterans want us to put the dollar sign on their patriotism, we can do it."[40]

Robertson maintained that she was terribly misquoted, and the article gave Democrats in her district something to use against her. She received letters from servicemen all over the country who were openly hostile to her because she questioned their patriotism or appeared to demean their service to the country. The animus toward her from servicemen and veterans' organizations continued to build as she prepared to run for a second term in the House. She returned to Muskogee in March of 1922 to appear before the local post of the American Legion for court-martial.[41] In a speech to the legionnaires she tried to explain her stand on the Bonus Bill. She repeated that the country could not afford the bill, but she did support aiding veterans when they needed assistance. "But I do want to make it clear that every man in this district who needs hospitalization or vocational training has only to lay this matter before me, and I'll promise him that I'll never rest until he has obtained them or until I am satisfied that there is no hope for his case," she said.[42] Undaunted, Robertson continued to voice her objections to the Soldiers' Bonus Bill. She was dismayed that she was only one of a few who voted according to conscience rather than to secure political popularity. She commented that most in the House did not want "to commit political suicide by voting against it whether we can afford it or not," and that she "cared more about the country than another term."[43] Robertson's outspoken manner and passion to defend what she believed to be right won her the admiration of members of Congress. One political columnist wrote that "Miss Alice has the respect and esteem of all the members regardless of their political affiliations. They would like nothing better than to aid her, if that were possible, and insure her a second term."[44]

Members of Congress respected the congresswoman for standing by her convictions and for her outspoken defense of her views. These very qualities, however, turned women's organizations against her, because Robertson was not a champion of many of the issues promoted by feminists. Many women believed that because Alice was a woman, her role in Congress would be to work toward the passage of women's legislation, regardless of whether it conflicted with Robertson's political philosophy and her concern for the greater good of the country. From the beginning of her tenure in Congress, Robertson fought against most of the legislation recommended by women's groups. She assailed the very concept of separate political organizations for women, especially the League of Women Voters and the National Woman's Party. At the NWP's convention in February 1922 she told Alice Paul, president of the NWP, and delegates who were called to vote on whether to continue the organization now that they had won suffrage, that it was in the best interest of women to abandon separate organizations and join one of the political parties.[45] In a speech before the Women's Press Club in Washington, Robertson delivered a similar message encouraging women to enter party politics and not engage in special interest politics. She informed her audience that she was not impressed with women's lobbying efforts and that, as a member of Congress, she "did not need a lobby to tell me how to vote."[46] Robertson believed that women could make a contribution to party politics. She explained to a Massachusetts gathering that women were needed at the lowest levels of the party organization, the precinct, where they could "make men interest themselves more" in politics and initiate a "cleaner" political environment.[47] One of the issues that alienated Alice from women's groups like the League of Women Voters was the congresswoman's stand on the Sheppard-Towner Maternity and Infancy Bill. Robertson believed that this first piece of social legislation, which was pending before the sixty-seventh Congress, would usurp the rights of individuals and establish what she considered a dangerous precedent of federal government paternalism.

The genesis of social welfare legislation emanated from reform-minded individuals of the late nineteenth-century progressive era. Florence Kelly, a Socialist and activist in the settlement house movement of the 1890s, conducted research on the working conditions of women and children who worked in the garment industry and sweatshops of urban America. Kelly's investigation prompted her to agitate for legislation that prohibited the labor of children under fourteen and mandated eight-hour workdays for women. After Kelly moved to New York City in 1899, she joined the National Consumer League and served on the National Child Labor Committee in 1904. Kelly and the women with whom she worked brought national attention to the problems encountered by women and children working in industrial America.[48] The information revealed in Kelly's investigation prompted the federal government to establish the Children's Bureau in the Department of Labor in 1912. Officials appointed Julia Lathrop, a coworker of Florence Kelly and fellow Socialist, as director. One of the Bureau's functions was to document the high rate of maternal and infant mortality. Field workers estimated that the rate of infant and maternal deaths was higher in the United States than in most other "civilized" countries. The conclusion was that low-income families needed instruction in maternal and infant hygiene.[49]

Lathrop initiated a study of how foreign countries handled the problem of health care for women and children of the working class. She concluded that most European countries offered three types of benefits for women and infants. In some countries, the state provided funds to cover the birth of the child. Others carried insurance, where companies collected money in advance from the state, from the individual, or from the employer. The third type of assistance was through volunteer agencies that provided nurses, but required the patient to absorb the costs. Lathrop concluded that the insurance systems in most European countries ultimately paid women on maternity leave fifty to seventy-five percent of their wages.[50] In 1917 Lathrop proposed congressional legislation to fund state programs for maternity and infant care. Federal action, however, was not taken on welfare legislation until after the passage of woman suffrage in 1920.

Robertson thought it her responsibility as a voting citizen and as a representative of the American people to safeguard society from legislation that could diminish American liberty. She maintained that there were certain powers in the Maternity Bill that had paternalistic capabilities of "incalculable dangers." She stated that "I am one of those millions

HARLOW'S WEEKLY
A Journal of comment and current events for Oklahoma
Victor E. Harlow, Editor

February 10,1923

Oklahoma Women in Politics
By Nelle Bunyan Jennings

The Oklahoma women are watching with renewed interest the different physical education and child welfare legislation bills slated to be adopted or rejected at this ninth legislature

The maternity bureau and child welfare bill known nationally as the Sheppard-Towner acceptance act is the factor in bringing to the capitol the leading club women of the state this week

This is the bill that passed the national congress Nov. 23, 1921, favoring the motherhood of the country, not because of the fact that Oklahoma had a woman congressman in the session but in spite to that fact, as Congressman Alice Robertson is known to have been greatly opposed to a motherhood bill. For this reason he women of Oklahoma are endeavoring to show just how much they do really need and want a health and welfare bill in this state and are going on record in the National Federation of Women's clubs as being unanimously in favor of the bill.

The bill was signed by President Harding in December, 1821, and up to June, 1922 twelve states had accepted the act by legislative action. Thirty had accepted it through their governor's action, pending the next meeting of their legislature. Four states, Louisiana, Massachusetts, New York, and Rhode Island, did not accept the Federal money.

of conservative home-loving women who never asked to vote, who dreaded new and heavy responsibilities. But God in His infinite wisdom placed upon us the burden of the suffrage. It matters not now whether we sought this duty or not. We cannot evade it and from cowardice or indolence we must not now fail our country." Robertson believed that it was much more preferable to allow "the family, the community, the municipality, and the state understanding local conditions to care for their own without national mandate or espionage."[51]

Robertson lectured that women who lobbied Congress, such as members of the LWV, were fighting for "class legislation of sex" and were playing on the sympathies of male members of Congress. She believed that the feminist argument that mothers wanted and needed this legislation would go unopposed in Congress because the congressmen would assume that women knew best on these matters. Robertson saw that women lobbyists were also able to intimidate congressmen with condemnation when they did not support the feminist view. While many congressmen avoided confrontation with organized women, Alice openly expressed her views and was not impressed with the "sob stuff" of those who championed the Maternity legislation. She allowed that she based her decision on this issue on weeks of prayer and a belief that she was doing the right thing. She was adamant that she would not let the feminists do her thinking for her. She was, after all, not a "representative of the women of America," but "She is an American Representative in Congress."[52] As such, she stood on the floor of the House and voiced her opposition to the Sheppard-Towner Bill. Testifying before the congressional committee, she informed the congressmen that women in Oklahoma were from pioneer stock and, therefore, knew how to bear a child and take care of children. It was, in other words, not the function of government. She also pointed out the tax burden imposed on Oklahomans who already experienced financial hardships, saying, "If we lay more taxes on our people, are we going to deprive the mothers and children of the food, the housing, the comforts they ought to have which they may not be able to have with the burden of taxation continuing to increase?"[53]

Alice not only raised the ire of women lobbyists with her defiance of their political activity, but she also antagonized the LWV back home in Muskogee, because she tried to defeat the Maternity Bill. In the summer of 1921, Alice wrote to Mrs. Phil Brown, president of the Oklahoma league, that she would like to have the opportunity to explain to women why she objected to the bill. She believed that once the ladies understood her reasoning, they would also understand the perceived dangers of the federal legislation. Mrs. Brown in turn sent Alice an official invitation to speak at the LWV state convention. But Robertson would not be the only speaker. Also invited to the meeting to offer an opposing view was Mrs. Maude Wood Park of New York, national president of the League of Women Voters, and her vice president, Mrs. Richard Edwards of Peru, Indiana. Robertson was on the defensive regarding her stand on the Sheppard-Towner Bill as well as other political decisions. In particular, Alice found herself defending her reluctance to support a woman as a member of the American Disarmament Committee. League women only thought it important that a woman be placed on the committee, but Robertson considered it essential to understand the political philosophy of the woman candidate. She would not make a commitment until she knew who the ladies had in mind. It was clear that Robertson doubted that she would agree with the political make-up of any woman endorsed by the league. The fire under which Robertson found herself was noted by the editor of the *Okmulgee Times*. In her defense, he berated women in the LWV as politicians who "were off on their usual campaign of vituperation, which as usual, is born of misinformation and ignorance." He accused women of devoting their time to "tea table and gossip exchange." The editor believed that Robertson had more than proved herself as politically capable and her "ability is recognized in such intellectual circles and not moved by whim and novelty of politics." He chastised the ladies for labeling Robertson as a political mishap.[54]

Robertson had other supporters in Oklahoma. In particular, many of the state's physicians were against the Maternity Bill, perhaps partly in fear that public health nurses would infringe on the physicians' responsibilities and care of patients. One Oklahoma doctor described the welfare legislation as "drastic and tyrannical." He maintained that it would take the freedom away from expectant mothers and that the bill was "Bolshevistic." The doctor recommended, "Why not introduce a bill to send this whole d--- bunch to Russia where they may get all they want of such Bolshevism, we don't want anything like that in America."[55] Robertson heard from women all over the country who supported her stand on the bill. Their letters carried the common message. "Please do not weaken on the account of the views of some in the League of Women Voters."[56]

After the Sheppard-Towner Bill passed both houses of Congress in 1921, women's groups in Oklahoma made plans for its implementation. By April the state received a $5,000 appropriation to begin the program. This allocation was used to write and disseminate the booklet "The Oklahoma Mothers' Baby Book." In May of 1922, Governor James Brooks Robertson appointed Miss Lula Hoagland as chief of the Bureau of Maternity and Infancy. The bureau under Hoagland's authority consisted of a director of public health, a health nurse, and a stenographer.[57] Eventually, Oklahoma received approximately $18,000 from the federal government with the stipulation that the state provide matching funds. As it turned out, the Sheppard-Towner Bill did not accomplish the goals set forth by its supporters. In Oklahoma from 1922 until 1924, the bureau conducted baby clinics, lectured to 24,000 mothers and taught childcare to 268 high school girls. By 1929, when Congress allowed the bill to expire, the only significant bureau activity in the state was the third annual baby rodeo, which was held at the Miller Brother's 101 Ranch near Ponca City.[58]

The League of Women Voters in Muskogee was so against Robertson that they planned to find another woman to run against her in the 1922 congressional elections. When a delegation went to Washington, they would not meet with the congresswoman. They called her a "traitor to her sex," and accused her of "playing with the men all the time." They were especially astounded that she would not even support an antismoking bill directed at women, which provided women with the slogan "She believes women should smoke but not vote." The animus directed at Robertson by women in such organizations as the League of Women Voters was not primarily due to her stand on the Sheppard-Towner Bill. The real issue was that she did not support a separate political identity for women. It was always the congresswoman's belief that constitutionally there was no sex, therefore, women could not claim certain rights.[59]

Robertson won the August 1922 primary and found herself once again running against W. W. Hastings in the November election. Lucky for Hastings, he won the election and regained his seat in the House. Alice returned to Muskogee, where, ironically, she began a new career as welfare director of the Muskogee Veterans' Hospital. Robertson lost the election for several reasons. Certainly, not adhering to the needs and concerns of her constituents was a factor; she lost the vote of the soldiers over her stand on the Bonus Bill and antagonized most women's groups with her antifeminist outlook. Another factor was the declining economic condition in Oklahoma while the Republicans were in office. The Democrats, along with the Farmer-Labor Reconstruction League, made a sweep of the state in the November 1922 election. Oddly enough, Robertson did not point to the above factors as instrumental in her defeat. Instead, she blamed the Ku Klux Klan, who in 1922 were just making their debut in Oklahoma.[60] Perhaps unknown to Robertson, the appearance of the Klan in the state coincided with a gradual waning of political activity among Oklahoma women. In 1923 many civic-minded women took a decisive turn to the right on the political spectrum when they found the Women of the Ku Klux Klan to be the organization that best represented their political ideals.

NOTES

1. *Harlow's Weekly*, 11 February 1921.
2. Samuel Austin Worcester is well known in American history for mission-ary work among the Cherokees in Georgia in the early nineteenth century. The state of Georgia believed that the troubles they were having with the Indians were because of the presence of whites within tribal lands. The state subsequently passed a law for the removal of all whites unless they had a permit, which was difficult to obtain. Worcester refused to abandon his work and was arrested and sentenced to four years in prison. He was released after the Supreme Court case of *Worcester v. Georgia* declared that the Georgia law was unconstitutional and ordered Worcester's release from prison. Bessie Allen Miller, "The Political Life of Alice M. Robertson," (master's thesis, University of Tulsa, 1946), p. 5; Linda Williams Reese, *Women of Oklahoma: 1890–1920*, (Norman: University of Oklahoma Press, 1997), p. 217.
3. Grant Foreman, "The Lady from Oklahoma," *The Independent* (26 March 1921): 311; James Vernol Clarke, "Presbyterian Woman in Congress," *New Era Magazine* (January 1921):24; Reese, *Women of Oklahoma: 1890–1920*, p. 217.
4. Miller, "The Political Life of Alice M. Robertson," p. 13.
5. Ibid, p. 15.
6. Grant Foreman, "The Hon. Alice M. Robertson," The *Chronicles of Okla-homa* 10 (1932):13; Reese, Woman of Oklahoma, 1890-1920, p. 219.
7. Francis Paul Prucha, *The Great Father, The United States Government and the American Indian*, (Lincoln: University of Nebraska Press, 1986), p. 202; *Proceedings of the Lake Mohonk Conference of the Indian*, (Lake Mohonk: Lake Mohonk Conference, 1892), p. 108.
8. Ibid.
9. *Proceedings of the Lake Mohonk Conference of the Indian*, p. 55.

10. For a overview of the shaping of Roosevelt's Indian program see William T. Hagan, *Theodore Roosevelt and Six Friends of the Indian*, (Norman: University of Oklahoma Press, 1997), p. 23.

11. Quoted from "A Woman Who Got into Congress through the Want-Ad Columns," *Literary Digest* (December 4, 1920): 56.

12. Lewis L. Gould, *The Presidency of Theodore Roosevelt*, (Lawrence: University of Kansas Press, 1991), pp. 7–8.

13. Theodore Roosevelt, *The Rough Riders*, (New York: Charles Scribners Sons, 1919), Appendices.

14. Miller, *The Political Life of Alice M. Robertson*, pp. 22–23.

15. Theodore Roosevelt to Alice Robertson, 8 January 1899, Theodore Roosevelt papers, microfilm, Bizzell Library, University of Oklahoma, Norman, Oklahoma. Hereafter cited TRP.

16. Theodore Roosevelt to secretary of the interior, 9 January 1899, TRP.

17. Miller, "The Political Life of Alice M. Robertson," p. 23; Grant Foreman, "The Lady From Oklahoma," p. 311.

18. Gould, *The Presidency of Theodore Roosevelt*, p. 8.

19. Ibid., p. 23.

20. Miller, "The Political Life of Alice Robertson," pp. 33, 41.

21. Ibid., p. 34; Ruth Moore Stanley, "Alice M. Robertson, Oklahoma's First Congresswoman," *Chronicles of Oklahoma* XLV, (1967): 2; Grant Foreman, "The Hon. Alice Robertson," *Chronicles of Oklahoma* XX, (1932):12; Maitreyi Mazumdar, "Alice's Restaurant: Expanding a Woman's Sphere," *Chronicles of Oklahoma* LXX (1992): 302; *Harlow's Weekly*, 13 August 1920.

22. Mazumdar, "Alice's Restaurant."

23. Thomas J. Jablonsky, *The Home, Heaven, and Mother Party: Female Anti-Suffragist in the United States, 1868–1920*, (Brooklyn: Carlson Publishing Inc., 1994), p. 2; Jan Jerome Camhi, *Women Against Women: American Anti-Suffragism 1880–1920*, (Brooklyn: Carlson Publishing Inc., 1994), p. 2.

24. Bernice Norman Crockett, "No Job for a Woman," *Chronicles of Oklahoma* LXI (1983): p. 148.

25. *Harlow's Weekly*, 10 June 1918.

26. A. D. Cochran to Alice Robertson, 12 March 1928, Alice M. Robertson Collection, Special Collection, McFarlin Library, University of Tulsa. Hereafter cited AMRCUT.

27. The contest to represent Oklahoma's second district in the United States Congress was among Robertson, Gus A. Tinch, R. A. Butts, and Orlando Swain. Tinch withdrew from the race, and Butts did little campaigning, preferring to stay in Colorado during the hot Oklahoma summer. *Harlow's Weekly*, 23 July 1920.

28. *Muskogee Daily Phoenix*, 13 October 1920.

29. There is no clue to the subject of her book. Reading between the lines one gets the impression that it was a history of her family. Alice Robertson to Dear Californians, 29 November 1920, Alice Robertson Collection, Oklahoma Historical Society, Oklahoma City; *Harlow's Weekly*, 19 November 1920. Hereafter cited ARCOHS.

30. Miller, "The Political Life of Alice M. Robertson," p. 50.

31. By today's political standards, Robertson would be a member of the religious right wing of the Republican party.

32. Mary C. Thaw to Mrs. Robertson, 25 January 1904, Thaw Correspondence AMRCUT.

33. Mary C. Thaw to Five and Others 3 August 1921; Thaw arranged for Robertson to obtain a non-interest loan from the Fidelity Title and Trust Company, Pittsburgh; P. S. Space to Alice Robertson 26 March 1921; Mary C. Thaw to Alice Robertson 30 January 1922.

34. *Harlow's Weekly*, 21 July 1921; Alice M. Robertson, "Present Economic Conditions as Affecting American Homes," p. 1, ARCOHS.

35. Alice Robertson to Ann Augusta Moore, 21 July 1921, ARCOHS.

36. Robertson, "Present Economic Conditions as Affecting American Homes," p. 6. ARCOHS.

37. *Harlow's Weekly*, 22 July 1921.

38. *Harlow's Weekly*, 27 May 1921; Miller, "The Political Life of Alice M. Robertson," p. 64.

39. Alice Robertson to Mary Thaw, 16 February 1922, AMRCUT.

40. Unidentified newspaper clipping, Ann Augusta Robertson Moore Collection, Oklahoma Historical Society, Oklahoma City, Oklahoma. Hereafter cited AARMOHS.

41. The court-martial was most likely a reprimand in line with her membership in the Woman's Auxiliary of the United Spanish War Veterans. *Harlow's Weekly*, 13 August 1920; Alice Robertson to Ann Augusta Robertson Moore, AARMOHS; The Ann Augusta Robertson Moore collection at the Oklahoma Historical Society contains numerous letters from World War I servicemen.

42. Unidentified newspaper clipping, 3 March 1922. AARMOHS.

43. Alice Robertson to Mary Thaw, 16 February 1922. AMRCUT.

44. Quoted in Miller, "The Political Life of Alice Robertson," p. 74.

45. *Harlow's Weekly*, 21 January 1921.

46. *Muskogee Times-Democrat*, n.d., clipping in AARMOHS.

47. *Harlow's Weekly*, 17 November 1921.

48. Robin Kadison Berson, *Marching to a Different Drummer: Unrecognized Heroes of American History*, (Connecticut: Greenwood Press, 1994), p. 159; J. Stanley Lemons, *Woman Citizen Social Feminism in the 1920s*, (Urbana: University of Illinois Press, 1973), pp. 153–154.

49. Lemons, *Woman Citizen*, p. 154.

50. Henry J. Harris, Maternity Benefit System Certain Foreign Countries, U.S. Department of Labor Children's Bureau, (Washington: Government Printing Office, 1919), pp. 11–13.

51. *Muskogee Times-Democrat*, n.d., in AARMOHS.

52. Unidentified newspaper article, AARMOHS.

53. U.S., Congress, House, A Bill for the Public Protection of Maternity and Infancy and Providing a Method of Cooperation Between the Government of the United States and The Several States, H.R. 2366, 67th Cong., 1st sess., 1921, p. 231.

54. Quoted in *Harlow's Weekly*, 26 August 1921.

55. Dr. L. H. Fouts to Lorraine Michael Gensman, Carl Albert Congressional Archives, University of Oklahoma, Norman, Oklahoma.

56. Sara Fletcher Wagner to Alice Robertson, 10 April 1921, AARMOHS.

57. *Harlow's Weekly*, 21 April 1922; 21 October 1922.

58. H. J. Darcy and Eula E. Fullerton, "Seventy-Five Years of Public Health in Oklahoma," a publication of the Oklahoma Department of Labor, 1964.

59. *Harlow's Weekly*, 4 May 1922.

60. During Alice Robertson's tenure in the House of Representatives, she sat on three committees: the Committee on Indian Affairs, the Committee on Expenditures in the Department of the Interior, and the Committee on Woman Suffrage. Robertson also introduced sixteen legislative bills. Out of this number, only two passed. Both were for an extension of time in building bridges across the Arkansas River at Fort Gibson and Webber Falls, Oklahoma. Miller, "The Political Life of Alice M. Robertson," pp. 50, 68, 81–83.

The Ultimate Patriots?
Oklahoma Women of
the Ku Klux Klan

By 1923 a number of conservative Oklahoma women moved their political activities out of the public arena and into the more private, unopposing sphere of secret sisterhood. The first public evidence of such a move was witnessed in Tulsa, Oklahoma, in February at the graveside services of Mrs. Mabel E. Southers. After friends and relatives left the ceremony, four hooded women in white robes and red capes emerged from a curtained automobile some two hundred feet from the gravesite. The four ladies marched over to the flower-banked casket of their departed friend and dropped three red roses onto it. With left hands over their hearts, the quartet returned to the waiting car and drove away. The mysteriously hooded ladies were members of the Knights of Kamelia, a patriotic society of conservative women who fought to maintain white supremacy and Protestant Christianity in the rapidly changing world of the 1920s.[1]

Women belonged to numerous patriotic organizations in the 1920s, but perhaps none as conservative as the Knights of Kamelia and the Women of the Ku Klux Klan (WKKK). What moved some women to expand their club membership to include such ultraconservative organizations as these is a difficult question to answer, especially with the paucity of records existing today for historians to investigate. But belonging to either one of these groups was an extreme measure and can be viewed as indicative of the anxiety women held for the welfare of the country in the postwar modernizing world of the 1920s. President Woodrow Wilson's programs to prepare Americans and America for involvement in the first World War and the effects of the war on American society had a direct impact on the conservative nature of many Americans in the 1920s. Wilson believed that Americans needed to be patriotic if they were going to support his war-preparedness programs. Especially important in creating patriotic citizens was teaching them that the American people were of one culture, and that culture was 100 percent American. From the Council on National Defense to the Food Conservation program to the Liberty Loan Drive, education through government-sponsored programs insisted that the American people demonstrate their patriotism and allegiance to the war cause. The aftereffects of these programs left unresolved hatreds and prejudices and a nativistic citizenry who believed that the German people were a threat to American institutions and that eastern European immigrants were suspects of un-American activities. After the war, Wilson's League of Nations and his ideals of a new world order and internationalism seemed at odds with the indoctrination the American people suffered during his war-preparedness programs. Upholding patriotism and rallying all people under the 100 percent American banner continued after the war, especially as more and more immigrants entered the country. Increased immigration from eastern Europe, whose people were religiously Catholic and many politically Socialist, was a threat to the ideal that America should only be a Protestant democratic society.[2]

The catalyst to bring about the phenomenal growth in ultraconservative organizations like the Ku Klux Klan in the early 1920s, however, was not only American prejudice toward people from eastern European countries, but also the emergence of a new postwar culture resulting from new technology and economic growth. Oklahomans experienced an economic boom in mineral-producing regions of the state, which also produced an increase in the state's population. From 1900 to 1920 the population of the state rose 123 percent. Economic prosperity and the creation of instant oil towns brought new people into the state, who thrived off of vice, crime, prostitution, and bootlegging. The new landscape of culturally and socially diverse people threatened the traditional culture of small town Oklahoma. Carter Blue Clark painted a picture of the economic boom and the resulting crime and vice in the oil-producing centers of the state in his study of the Ku Klux Klan in Oklahoma:

> Residents of Tulsa could drive to the outskirts of town to Joe Baker's road house. It was a converted farmhouse just off the road with a wire fence around it and a guard at the gate. Baker's place was only one of thirty in the vicinity to choose from. Thirty-five cents bought a pint of black beer. More money could be spent on slot machines or on the women who sat around the bar. There were always fifteen to twenty cars there day or night, usually carrying oil field roustabouts

or laborers from the city. The roadhouses were the scenes of nightly shootings and drunken brawls which alarmed the quieter residents of the area. If they desired, the revelers could drive into Tulsa to one of the fourteen bordellos in the district reserved for them in 1921. They could also drive to one of the fifty gambling spots in the town. If they wanted something stronger than alcohol, they could visit one of the thirty narcotic dens.[3]

Many Oklahomans saw little value in the changes taking place in their society, especially when lawlessness seemed to rule instead of order and justice. Resorting to vigilantism to keep law and order was a frontier tradition and perhaps an easy tradition to once again practice considering the perceived cultural decay. Oklahoma women, like many of their husbands, brothers, and fathers, found the Ku Klux Klan the ideal post from which to fight for a conservative nation of white, Protestant, 100 percent Americans who believed in the continuance of traditional Victorian values that embraced motherhood, home, and family.

The Ku Klux Klan of the 1920s was an updated version of the Klan that Confederate General Nathan Bedford Forrest organized after the Civil War. In 1866 General Forrest called together ten of his fellow officers to establish a social organization in Pulaski, Tennessee. The men called their club the Kuklos, which in Greek means *circle*. The name was indicative of the planned mysterious nature of the organization. Kuklos was derived from the Greek Cyclades, which was one of two islands off the coast of Greece, the other being Sporades, which meant, "to scatter." Klansmen liked the name Kuklos because it signified a feeling of warm comradery among friends.[4] The circle of friends eventually grew into a vigilante-type terrorist group whose goal it was to protect white society after the Civil War from carpetbaggers, scalawags, and freedmen. Especially important was the protection of Southern white women from the influences of black men. After the Civil War, white men believed that they no longer had exclusive rights to white women, especially if freed black men obtained equal rights and suffrage. White men, who viewed women as "sexual acquisitions" feared that women would be overpowered by black men and forced into marriage.[5] So, in order to protect Southern womanhood, Klan members committed acts of violence on many unsuspecting and innocent people throughout the South during Reconstruction. In defense of Klan violence, General Forrest testified in 1871 before the United

HARLOW'S WEEKLY

A Journal of comment and current events for Oklahoma

Victor E. Harlow, Editor

November 24, 1921

A Moral Awakening In Oklahoma
Ku Klux Klan Active

The situation in Carter County has resulted in activity on the part of the Ku Klux Klan which through the medium of the advertisement in the *Daily Admoreite* has warned all "gambles, bootleggers, hi-jackers, gunmen, loafers lawbreakers of every class and description, black and white," to leave the city. The Shawnee News referring to the Carter county situation says:

A carnival of feuds, murders, drunken debauches, open operation of gambling and bootlegging joints, has existed with rare interruptions since the cooling off of the people following the ending of the war. Russell Brown, the former county attorney addressing the mass meeting, said he knew and the sheriff and district judge knew, that juries were not regularly drown. He could have gone further and said that it has been the practice to frame cases by fixing the witnesses and to insure acquittals—or convictions—according to how the gang felt about the defendant in the case, frequently verdicts having been brought in of not guilty on the ground of self defense when the man murdered had no weapon and was deliberately shot down.

Admore's political and criminal system has been so closely interwoven with the operation of business for a generation that it has been difficult to secure action and only now it is possible because of the influx of new people who insist on making it a safe and decent place to live and who have not compromised themselves one time or another with the political-criminal element dominating the affairs of the country.

The Ada News Commenting upon the fact that the Ku Klux Klan is attempting to take the situation in hand, says"

The *Ardmorite* carries a page ad over the Ku Klux Klan signature warning law breakers of ever description to make themselves scarce in Carter County. Carter county citizens have been much aroused lately by a wave of lawlessness. This affords the Ku Klux Klan a fine opportunity to clean up the county and the result of their aid will be watched with interest. If the order makes good in this case it will go a long way towards silencing its critics. Whether tar and feathers are applied or evidence furnished the authorities upon which the roughs can be put behind the bars, results are what the public wants to see.

States Senate that the Klan's actions were justified because "ladies were ravished by some of these negroes, who were tried and put in the penitentiary but were turned out in a few days afterward."[6] Ultimately, the Klan of the Reconstruction South died out. In 1869 General Forrest disbanded the organization because he and the founding members considered many of the new recruits undesirable. Also, the United States Congress passed legislation that banned the Klan and declared their intimidating tactics, especially their propensity to don a disguise when seeking out evildoers, unlawful.[7]

In the intervening years between Reconstruction and the first World War, Southerners held a romantic notion that Klansmen had saved the integrity of Southern society. In 1915 the stories and the memories of this "romantic period" in Southern history were brought to the big screen in D. W. Griffith's motion picture *The Birth of a Nation*. The movie, which premiered in Atlanta, Georgia, on Thanksgiving night, advanced a patriotic portrayal of the Civil War and Reconstruction and a nostalgic depiction of hooded, white-robed Klansmen riding to save the South from Yankees and freedmen. Ironically, at the same time that Georgians were in the theater remembering the glory days of the Ku Klux Klan, a cross burned high atop Stone Mountain, outside Atlanta, announcing the re-organization of the white supremacy organization. On December 4, 1915, the state of Georgia granted the new society a charter, which officially launched "The Invisible Empire, Knights of the Ku Klux Klan, Inc." The founder of the twentieth century's version of the Reconstruction Klan was William Joseph Simmons, minister in the Methodist Episcopal church, circuit rider, and fraternal organizer. It was through the later occupation that Simmons came to reestablish the KKK. He was successful in organizing the Woodmen of the World and other societies, in which he was an active member. In all, he held a degree of membership in the Masons, Knights of Pythias, the Odd Fellows, and the Woodmen. He was the ideal person to organize a new fraternal organization patterned after the Klan of yesteryear. Evidently, as a child Simmons had read extensively about the Ku Klux Klan of the Reconstruction era and was especially enthralled with what he viewed as the heroic efforts of Southern Klansmen to save white supremacy and Southern womanhood during the perilous days following the Civil War. He envisioned a new Klan that would be a "living memorial" to the heroic efforts of Reconstruction-era Klansmen. Like many fraternal organizations of the day, the Klan followed certain rituals. But Simmons made the Klan more distinctive by enveloping it in deeper

secrecy and mystery than the original Klan and insisting on a strange nomenclature that overutilized the letter K.[8]

Growth of the Klan was slow under Simmons's leadership. He was
only successful in establishing the order in Georgia and the neighboring
state of Alabama. During the first World War, recruitment slowed and ultimately changed the focus of the Klan. Like many citizens during the war,
Simmons volunteered his time for the cause. He joined the Citizens Bureau
of Investigation in Atlanta, where he became a citizen spy. Simmons subsequently sanctioned spying as an acceptable method used by Klansmen
to observe the behavior of fellow citizens. By so doing, Simmons changed
the Klan from a fraternal order that believed in white male supremacy
and the good old days of Reconstruction to a secret, moralistic, patriotic
organization, whose goal it was to police society. Klan membership during
the war years did not exceed 6,000. But Klan fortunes changed after the
war, when Simmons met Edward Young Clark and Elizabeth Tyler of the
Southern Publicity Association. Simmons hired the Association to promote the Klan and build its membership. Clark and Tyler immediately set
to work. They divided up the states into subdivisions (provinces) and sent
1,100 solicitors (Kleagles) into the field. Klan headquarters instructed the
Kleagles to integrate the prejudices of the people in any given region into
Klan programs in hopes of boosting membership. The Southern Publicity
Association increased membership in the Klan substantially and raised
significant funds to pay Clark and Tyler their percentage and to rein-
vest the remainder into the membership campaign. From June 1920 to
October 1921, Klan membership rose to around 100,000 men. From the
required ten dollars (Klectoken) membership fee, the Klan took in more
than $1,500,000. The geographical boundaries of the Klan also increased
to include states in the Midwest, Southwest, and Pacific Coast.[9]

Oklahoma ranked high in Klan membership and had the distinction of having the most successful Klan organization in the Southwest.
This was partly due to the nature of Oklahoma settlement. Many who
migrated to Oklahoma were from the old South, where their culture read-
ily accepted the ideals of the post–Civil War Klan. In fact, many of the
original Klansmen lived in Oklahoma, and like veterans of foreign wars,
they still had their Klan regalia, which they wore or loaned to others to
use on special occasions. Klansmen also made appearances in Oklahoma
before the official founding of the order at Stone Mountain. One such
appearance was at a Liberty Loan drive in Skiatook. Evidently, there
were several men in the community who some considered unpatriotic

because they were hesitant to purchase government bonds to support the war. News of such un-American sympathies reached the Klan. When the Liberty Bond parade was making its way down main street, sixteen Klansmen, or Kluxers, rode their horses over the hill leading into town and joined the procession. They carried banners that warned slackers that the Kluxers had ropes waiting for those who did not show their patriotism by buying bonds.[10]

The national Klan organization did not officially organize in Oklahoma until the summer of 1920, when two Kleagles arrived in Oklahoma City to begin recruiting. One way in which to find prospective members was through fraternal organizations like the Masons. In fact, it was in the Masonic Halls in Oklahoma where the new order held its first meetings. Klansmen also met in Oklahoma City at the Congregational Church and the old Epworth University building. Besides raiding fraternal orders for members, Kleagles also targeted those who served on the wartime Council of Defense. Kleagles figured correctly that many on the council had gained useful experience in detecting unpatriotic citizens and wartime slackers. The thought was that council members had the qualities of an ideal Klansman. After the initial membership drive in Oklahoma City, Kleagles moved to Tulsa to set up a similar network of recruitment. From both major cities, Kleagles broadened the membership drive into smaller Oklahoma communities.[11] Originally, the Ku Klux Klan of the 1920s, like its nineteenth-century predecessor, was an all-male fraternity. It was a secret patriotic organization that was anti-Catholic, anti-Semitic, anti-Communist, and anti–foreign immigration. Klansmen were also the guardians of society's morality and virtue. But guarding society's morality was traditionally within women's sphere, and for that reason perhaps, the Klan held great appeal to many Oklahoma women in the 1920s.

The opportunity to develop a women's ultraconservative organization with Klan-like features resulted from a power struggle within the Klan between promoters, Tyler and Clark, and founder, Simmons. Elizabeth Tyler, especially, had amassed significant power and authority. A congressional investigation into Klan activities inadvertently reinforced what many had feared; that the Klan was under the influence of a woman. Simmons, fearing loss of his authority, devised a plan to inaugurate a new Klan organization especially for women. Perhaps to sidetrack Tyler from usurping his authority, Simmons appointed her to oversee implementation of a women's organization. Tyler acquiesced and immediately found five hundred women throughout the country who wanted membership in an organization that opposed "Jews, Catholics, Negroes, Socialists, and radicals." Tyler did not plan for the women's organization to be an auxiliary to the men's order, but its own entity, equal to the Knights. Her efforts to organize a women's order eventually failed.[12]

Simmons also had competition for control of the Klan from Hiram Wesley Evans, a Dallas dentist, and a new Klan recruit. Evans offered to organize for Texas if he could incorporate into the Klan program many of the ideals of his fraternal organization, the Masons. Evans became the first Exalted Cyclops of Dallas Klan no. 66. In 1922 he was promoted to district leader (Great Titan) and quickly climbed the Klan hierarchical ladder. Simmons appointed him national secretary (Imperial Kligrapp), a position that allowed Evans access to more and more power and the leadership position. Evans worked his way into the office of temporary Imperial Wizard when Simmons took some time away from his duties to recover from alcoholism. During Simmons's recovery, Evans suggested that Simmons resign his post. Simmons agreed, but only because he believed that once recovered, he would continue to lead the Klan. While Simmons was out of the picture, Evans ousted Clark and Tyler and took over complete control of the organization, leaving Simmons with only a ceremonial position as Emperor. Once back on his feet, Simmons tried to gain back control of the Klan by once again initiating a separate women's organization. Like those in other political organizations in the early 1920s, Simmons realized that women were an untapped resource. Not only would they constitute a significant membership, but also they would add revenue for the organizational efforts.[13] One of the methods used by Simmons to recruit women into his new order was to tap into women's patriotic organizations that were becoming more and more prevalent by 1923. His first success was in Oklahoma, where he formed an alliance with a study group in Bartlesville called the White American Protestant (W.A.P.) study club, an organization with chapters in Tulsa, Claremore, and other eastern Oklahoma communities. Simmons called his new organization the Kamelia and appointed himself El Magus (leader).[14]

Women moved quite easily from their patriotic clubs into a secret organization because, from behind the mask of anonymity, they believed they could better enforce traditional American values. Even before William Simmons organized the Kamelia, Oklahoma women, like many women across the country, had already incorporated into their clubs similar rituals and ideals of the Klan. For example, in November 1923 in Atlanta, Georgia, three hundred women marched in white robes and masks. Commentators assumed that the women were from an auxiliary of the Ku Klux Klan. The ladies were quick to point out that their organization was the Dixie Protestant Women's Political League, and their end was to work toward "clean" politics. They admitted that the masks protected them in this endeavor, but anonymity also helped them in their mission. "We can find out more about politics that way," one marcher commented.[15] Ultraconservative women's organizations in the Southwest that resembled the Klan included the Order of American Women in Fort Worth, Texas, the Ladies of the Invisible Empire in Louisiana and Arkansas, and the Ladies of the Cu Clux Clan in Oklahoma.[16]

The seat of activity for the Klan and women's patriotic organizations was in eastern Oklahoma, especially around Tulsa. The tide of 100 percent Americanism ran strong in Tulsa, as did the vice and crime. Tulsa also had a history of racial violence. Lynching blacks was openly practiced, and much of the black district was burned after a 1921 race riot, where more than thirty blacks were killed. There was an atmosphere of lawlessness, and when law and order could not be maintained in Tulsa, vigilantism reigned.[17] It is not surprising, then, that a women's patriotic organization called the Cu Clux Clan made its debut in Sand Springs, a community adjacent to Tulsa, in February 1923. In that month, six women in masks and white robes marched up the aisle of the Methodist church during a revival meeting. The women's mission was to announce that they would "help" the Klan in an effort to rid City Hall of corruption. Evidently, the women suspected a bootlegging operation in the highest levels of city government. They informed the parishioners that the women would "find where some of our city officials are keeping enough booze stored to have more than enough for themselves."[18] Clanswomen took on the responsibility of upholding the eighteenth amendment to the U.S. constitution, which made it illegal to manufacture or sell alcoholic beverages in the United States. The women believed that prohibition aided personal liberty and promoted the "full use of our faculties." The problem was that the amendment was difficult to enforce, especially in oil-boom regions of the Southwest such as Oklahoma. Klan officials instructed their members that it was important to society that prohibition be fully enforced. If not, then there would be a growing disrespect for the law and an opening for further "evil" to occur.[19] Clanswomen were so impassioned with the prohibition cause that it was not unusual for them to "raid" bootlegging operations and destroy the equipment. On one occasion, Clanswomen from

Oklahoma City destroyed the still of one enterprising individual who set up his operation south of the city.[20]

The women liked to use the element of surprise to gain attention for their cause. They also employed threats and intimidation to win demands. Their typical method of operation was to don their masks and white robes and make a dramatic appearance at some public event, where they announced their purpose. It was also a common occurrence to find that the ladies had left a list of their demands at some public place, like the high school in Henryetta, Oklahoma. There the ladies of the W.A.P. study club entered one of the schools after hours and left for school board officials a letter that enumerated the ladies' wishes. The Ku Klux Klan had made a previous visit to the school insisting that teachers incorporate into their lesson plans a period for Bible study. Women of the W.A.P. study club followed up the Klan visit with further recommendations for the curriculum. They believed that the core of instruction should consist of 100 percent Americanism, and "morality and virtue in every sense, and in the Word of God." The ladies also declared that they would not stand for "flapper" teachers in the schools, and that school officials should "no longer or in the coming term employ a girl with her dress to her knees, bobbed hair, and painted face." The ladies warned that "we are a great number of Americans and are powerful here in Henryetta. Don't disregard this."[21]

Simmons found the W.A.P. study club the ideal organization in Oklahoma with which to build his Knights of Kamelia. He started off his campaign for membership by organizing a three-day Tri-State convention on April 18, 1923, in Tulsa. More than two thousand women from Oklahoma, Kansas, and Missouri attended the convention. The proceedings of the three-day affair were held in secret, but the highlight of the event for Tulsans was the parade on the last day of the meeting. For the occasion, Simmons ordered robes for the ladies, which he designed. They were white "flowing" gowns with a vivid red K on the left shoulder and capes and hoods to protect the women's identity. Newspapers estimated that there were 30,000 to 40,000 people who watched 500 women march for 19 blocks on a cold, damp, gray day in April. They paraded eight across and carried little red schoolhouses, which, they maintained, symbolized the home. The women also carried banners that advertised who they were and the principles for which they stood. The banners read "Kamelia," "Protection of Women," "This group is 100 percent Americanism," and the most interesting of them all, "Kiss the Flag or Cross the Pond."[22]

Simmons's Knights of Kamelia had only a few months of organizational lead-time before Klan leader Hiram Evans recognized there were benefits to including women in Klan membership. The Klan also understood that the most effective method of recruitment would be through women's patriotic associations. In June of 1923, Klan officials invited administrative heads from women's patriotic clubs to meet in Washington, D.C., to discuss the possibility of establishing a Klan organization for women. At the meeting, the women approved the constitution and laws of the Women of the Ku Klux Klan, thereby formally inaugurating the new group. The national headquarters was in Little Rock, Arkansas. Mrs. Lula A. Markwell was the first Imperial Commander and Miss Robbie Gill was the Imperial Kligrapp, or secretary.[23] What distinguished the WKKK from the Kamelia was the practice of secrecy. Simmons's Knights of Kamelia insisted on anonymity, whereas the WKKK, like its male counterpart, was more open and less mysterious.[24]

In all, there were more than fifty-nine orders of the Women of the Ku Klux Klan in Oklahoma. It is difficult to compile a composite of the typical Klanswoman. Basically, members included women from a broad spectrum of interests, including political activists and those involved in party politics. Membership cards for the WKKK in Cherokee, Oklahoma, reveal some interesting characteristics. For one, not all women believed that their place was in the home, although they fought for the traditional values of home and family. At least one-third of the members listed a profession other than housewife. The range of occupations included stenographer, milliner, teacher, nurse, funeral director, and farmer. Women were also active in clubs other than the Klan. The most favored was the Order of the Eastern Star, the women's auxiliary to the Freemasons. The Masons were a fraternal order established in Oklahoma before statehood in 1907. By the 1920s, there were Masonic Halls in most Oklahoma towns, including a three-million-square-foot temple in Guthrie.[25] Members of the Masons and the Order of the Eastern Star held similar views to men and women who belonged to the Klan. In particular, both the Masons and the Klan were anti-Catholic and fought to keep Catholics from holding public office and establishing private school education.[26] The Eastern Star was organized similarly to he WKKK in that the hierarchy of officers had regimental-type titles. The head of the state organization was the Grand Matron and below her was the Deputy Matron. The secretary was the Grand Secretary and the order was the Grand Chapter. In 1921 the Grand Secretary reported that membership in 291 state chapters was

23,859, a gain of 3,898 for the year.[27] More than one-half of the Klansmen in the Cherokee Klan belonged to the Eastern Star. Also noted on the membership cards were the religions of the prospective members, plus those of their husbands, fathers, and mothers. Of course, being Protestant was one of the initial requirements of Klan membership. The Klan did not care if a person did not belong to a particular Protestant religion, but recommended that those who listed their faith as Christian find membership in a church.[28]

The records from the Coalgate Klan no. 63 provide an even richer source in which to ascertain the characteristics of an Oklahoma Klanswoman. Like the women in the Cherokee Klan, Coalgate Klanswomen were members of the Eastern Star and held professional positions. Mrs. T. P. Cardwell serves as an example. Mrs. Cardwell was Tag Agent for Coal County, Oklahoma. She was a member of the Methodist church, the most predominant church among Klan members. Besides her membership in the Eastern Star, where she held the position of Grand Matron, she belonged to the Neighbors of Woodcraft, Chamber of Commerce, Pythian Sisters, and General Federation of Women's Clubs. Although Klan literature stressed that women should hold no allegiance to a political party, a majority of Klanswomen belonged to the Democrat party. Mrs. Cardwell was precinct committeewoman for the party. Cardwell also held leadership positions in civic groups where she worked to improve her community. She was chairman of the Child Welfare League, supervisor of the Red Cross, and worked on various support committees during the first World War. Other women in the Coalgate Klan had similar profiles to Cardwell. What is striking is that women assumed leadership positions in various organizations and were active politically in the Democrat party.[29]

Klan membership was not open to every woman, only those who met stringent qualifications set down by the organization. The usual manner of recruitment was for a Klanswoman to approach prospective members by offering them invitation cards referred to as the "Patriotic Call." The ladies only offered the card to women who were native-born American citizens and owed no allegiance to any "foreign government, political party, sect, creed, or ruler." The invitation card listed the characteristics thought important in a good Klanswoman, "tenets of the Christian religion, just laws and liberty, upholding the constitution of the United States, preventing the causes of mob violence and lynching, limitation on foreign immigration, and to understand the relations of home and duty." If a woman who received the "Patriotic Call" wanted to accept this invitation to apply for membership, she presented the card at the next meeting of the WKKK. She then could fill out her paperwork and submit an official application. Klan officials investigated the information offered by the applicant to verify that she was a white native-born Christian and loyal to the government of the United States.[30]

The Women of the Ku Klux Klan was a well-disciplined society with military overtones. The president of the WKKK was called Excellent Commander or General. The Excellent Commander's territory was the Klanton for which she issued orders, formulated rules, and assigned duties. The second in command was the Major, who saw to the execution of the General's orders. Captains maintained the Klanton and Lieutenants took care of the precincts. But, under this form of leadership, Klanswomen still formed political committees that were similar to other women's clubs in the 1920s; Americanization, Public Schools, Public Amusement, Legislation, Child Welfare, Juvenile Delinquency, Citizenship, Civic Affairs, Law Enforcement, and Peace and Politics. As in most clubs, committees served to educate women of societal issues.[31] Ritual was an important part of the Klan organization, perhaps encouraging discipline, and allegiance to the order. Every meeting began with the SOK or the Sign of the Klanswomen. Women raised their left arms, held their thumbs in the palms of their hands, spread fingers out, and put their left feet forward. From this position they moved into the SOL, or the Sign of Loyalty. While reciting "My head, my heart, and my hand, for God and home and native land," the ladies touched their foreheads with fingers of the left hand, then touched their hearts. In the last gesture of the ritual, they straightened out their hands, elbows at waistline, palms upward. It certainly must have been a challenge to many women to not only memorize a new language where most words started with the letter K, but to memorize ceremonial rituals, where leadership was sure to scrutinize performance.[32]

The disciplined ritualistic nature of the organization was attractive to women and offered them a definition of themselves that perhaps they could not find as members of society outside of the Klan. For one, the structure offered women the opportunity to demonstrate individual effort and the ability and to improve their status. By their own talents, women could climb up the hierarchical structure to assume positions of responsibility. Klanswomen also believed that they were equal to men, at least in God's eyes. Klan literature from the Women of the Ku Klux Klan headquarters in Little Rock emphasized to women that their purpose was indeed inspired by God and that in God's kingdom they were equal, if not superior, to men.[33]

Klanswomen held the same views as their male counterparts in the Ku Klux Klan about what constituted a good society. They were white supremacists who stood against foreign immigration, internationalism, and Roman Catholicism. The Klan considered people from European countries, whose political systems and religious orientations opposed democracy and Christianity, to be a threat to American institutions. For the Klan leadership, it went without saying that Christianity was synonymous with Protestantism. Catholics were seldom seen as Christians or even desirable members of the Republic. Indeed, Klan members believed that the Roman Catholic church was a threat to America. Klansmen and Klanswomen maintained that the founding fathers "meant for America to be Anglo-Saxon and Protestant." However, by the 1920s, the Klan calculated that the leading denomination in thirty-one of the forty-eight states was Catholic. To the Klan, this was more than the spread of Catholicism, but the growth of "the greatest political force in America" and this force was better organized than any other political entity. The Klan believed that the reason for the growth of Catholicism was the "mass" European immigration, which continued with little objection from most Americans. "While we slept, Rome poured a flood tide of her followers through our gate of immigration," wrote one Klansman. The thought was that the increase of Catholic immigrants into the country enhanced the power of the Catholic church. The solution was to organize a united Protestant force in which the Klan would play a major role. "The Klan comes, like a white prophet from the wilderness, crying: Let all who are on the Lord's side rally to the Fiery Cross and for Christ, and country, for home, hope, and heaven."[34] Especially alarming to the Klan was the spread of Catholic institutions, particularly schools and hospitals. The Klan put its political energy behind supporting the separation of church and state, and wholeheartedly supported public school education. But the Klan did not believe that separation of church and state precluded teaching of the Bible in the public schools. To the contrary, teaching from the Bible was as American as apple pie. Klansmen also believed that women could play an important role in promoting and maintaining a Protestant nation. Piety was, after all, one of the tenets of being a good Victorian woman and an important aspect of women's role as moral guardians of society.[35]

The Ultimate Patriots? Oklahoma Women of the Ku Klux Klan

Roman Catholics were only one group targeted by the Klan in a wider condemnation of the "Cosmopolitan movement," which encompassed religious and politically diverse groups of people throughout the world. It was the philosophies of these people, "Universalism, Sovietism, Communism, Socialism, Anarchism, Judaism, and Roman Catholicism," that the Klan considered a threat to Americanism. Klan members also believed that there were four different types of people who particularity wanted to destroy the "American group mind." Men and women of the Klan viewed the Jews as a people who would never fit into the character of Americanism because the Jewish people maintained their own culture and would not accept the "one-mindedness necessary to true nationalism." The other three groups of people—the Celts, the Mediterranean people, and the Alpine people (peasant class in Europe)—were all associated with the Roman Catholic church, and therefore, they could never be true Americans.[36] The Bolsheviks and their infliction of a dictatorship saw the proof that people with different philosophies and of different religions could be destructive to the ideals of Americanism in the takeover of Russia on the Russian people. The new regime in Russia opposed democracy, which the Klan believed was the "best form of government yet discovered by mankind," and the Soviets opposed the Christian religion. "They teach their children that all religion is but a capitalistic opiate to quiet the sorrows of the proletariat," said a Klansman. It was up to the Klan to stop the spread of communism, to meet it head on, and to make sure it did not find fertile soil in the United States.[37] Women could play a role in this fight to protect American institutions by being patriotic and devout Christians. But also, like their fellow Klansmen, their job was to help fight moral decay and improve the condition of mankind. The thought was that if men and women and the American family were happy, content, and well fed, they would hold allegiance to democracy and 100 percent Americanism and not look to other systems of government as a solution to their problems. Oklahoma Klanswomen played a significant role in this cause.

Working for the welfare of others was an important part of the WKKK program. In what some referred to as their "Guardian Angel" role, Klanswomen helped those in their communities by providing necessary items such as clothing, food baskets, and in some cases money. A family in need very seldom saw its benefactor. If folks were behind in their rent, money would mysteriously be found on the doorstep. Those who could not afford groceries found a basket of food.[38] Klanswomen also helped to sup-

137

port public institutions that housed the poor and United States Veterans of War. The two hundred women who belonged to the Muskogee Klan No. 16 established a day nursery, and helped to furnish a living room for citizens at the "poor farm," and provided fried chicken dinners for the veterans at the Muskogee Veterans Hospital. Other charitable acts of the Muskogee Klanswomen included providing food, clothing, and rent for thirty-four families and outfitting school children in decent clothes so that their apparent poverty would not hinder their efforts to obtain an education.[39]

Many women who joined the Klan were not as politically active as women who entered the political arena through their work in political parties, clubwork, and political action organizations. But this did not mean that Klanswomen were apolitical. For the most part, their politics were the politics of the Klan, and they followed Klan dictum when casting their votes on issues and candidates. But Klanswomen also took an active role in political campaigns if the stakes were high, which was the case in the presidential race of 1927. The presidential contest was between Republican Herbert Hoover, a Midwestern native-born Protestant, and New York's governor, Alfred E. Smith, who was the son of Catholic immigrants. It was the contention of the Klan that Al Smith, if elected, would not be able "to harmonize the laws of his church with the laws of his country where the two conflict." Not only did Smith's immigrant roots and Catholicism alarm Klanswomen, but also his position to overturn the Eighteenth Amendment on prohibition demonstrated that the governor was not a patriotic American. The prohibition issue and Smith's connection with the tobacco trust, which had launched an advertising campaign directed at women, inspired many Klanswomen to work actively to defeat Smith. Klanswomen also supported tightening immigration laws to stem the flow of Catholics from eastern Europe. They pointed to the Sacco and Vanzetti case, in which two Italian immigrant anarchists were on trial for murdering a guard and paymaster in South Braintree, Massachusetts. Even though there was not sufficient evidence to convict the two, they were executed in August 1927. To Klanswomen, Sacco and Vanzetti served as evidence of the sort of undesirable immigrants that were entering the United States and reinforced Klan resolve to fight for tighter immigration laws.[40]

Local politics were also important to Oklahoma Klanswomen, especially in a state where the Klan assumed so much political power. In the early 1920s the Klan, under the leadership of Grand Dragon N. Clay

Jewett, was the most powerful political force in the state. Although the Klan resorted to night riding, intimidation, and violence as a way to reform society, they realized that to change the system they had to gain control of politics. By voting Klansmen into political offices in the state, the Klan would be able to control the growing crime and corruption of public officials and law enforcement agencies, stem the flow of immigrants into the state, and rid society of radicals and grafters. In the 1920s, candidates running for office had very little chance of success unless they had the Klan's endorsement. Of the 125 state legislators, sixty-eight were affiliated with the Ku Klux Klan. The political power of the Klan was perhaps seen most significantly in the impeachment of Oklahoma Governor John Callaway Walton in 1923.

Walton began to disappoint those who elected him to the governorship soon after he assumed office in 1923. He passed out few "political plums" to those who helped him win the election. Instead, he appointed his friends to positions that were not very rewarding, and amongst these appointees there were repeated scandals and arguments over the "spoils of office." Walton's opponents believed that he abused the power of his office with the appointment of unqualified individuals to state positions. Walton was also fiscally extravagant. He alarmed legislative conservatives when he allocated large sums of money to friends and cronies. In some cases, he appointed people who never occupied the office but received monthly paychecks anyway. By July 1923, Democrats were starting to talk about the possibility of impeaching the governor because of his general incompetence and the corruption in his administration. The impeachment battle, however, did not gain momentum until Walton decided he needed to take action against the vigilantism and wanton violence administered at the hands of the Ku Klux Klan. Throughout the state, violence between Klan and anti-Klan forces caused many innocent people to suffer undo cruelty.[41] The incidents of violence that were brought to Walton's attention left the governor with very little recourse but to take action. In one particular incident, anti-Klansmen carried a Tulsa man's mutilated body to the state capital for Walton to see. An inquiry in Tulsa into the beating revealed that the weapon used was a "whip made from a shortened baseball bat, with shoe-leather and a wire attached." In another incident, Klansmen castrated a prominent minister's son and dumped him on his father's front porch in Oklahoma City.[42]

To bring an end to the reign of terror imposed by the Klan in Tulsa and other eastern Oklahoma counties, Walton imposed martial law in

September 1923. Oklahoma guardsmen took up positions in Tulsa and surrounding communities to protect Oklahoma citizens. The more Walton tried to stop Klan violence by imposing martial law in communities that seemed to have little law enforcement, the more members of the state legislature talked of impeaching the governor. Campbell Russell, Walton's political opponent, and a Klansmen, circulated a petition to place an initiative on the ballot in the October special election that, if passed by the people, would allow legislators to call a special session to impeach a governor.[43] The state constitution, however, stipulated that only the governor had the power to call a special session. By September 15, 1923, Walton had issued a declaration of martial law throughout the state. Five days later, sixty-five legislators met at the Skirvin Hotel in Oklahoma City where they issued a proclamation calling the legislature into a special session to talk about impeachment of the governor. The governor, in abeyance of the state constitution, sent state troopers into the capital to discourage legislators from calling a special session on September 26. The lawmakers disbanded. This was only a temporary setback. In the October election, the citizens of Oklahoma overwhelming passed the initiative allowing the legislators to call a special session to impeach the governor.[44]

Walton recovered quickly from his impeachment from Oklahoma's highest office. And, not one to be deterred by bad publicity, Walton gathered support to wage a new political campaign for the United States Senate. His run for the Senate further split the Democrat party in the state into pro-Walton/anti-Walton factions. At the head of the anti-Walton group was a conservative member of the Democrat party, Mrs. O. H. Cafky, of Forgan. Mrs. Cafky was vice-chairman of the Oklahoma Democrat Central Committee and had the full support of the Ku Klux Klan. But Klan endorsement did not necessarily mean that Cafky belonged to the WKKK. In fact, she denied any affiliation to the secret organization. She did, however, belong to conservative groups whose members filled the WKKK roster. In all, Mrs. Cafky was a member of the Order of the Eastern Star, the Rebekahs, DAR, and the American Legion Auxiliary.[45] Mrs. Cafky was significant in the Klan's fight against Walton because she broke ranks from the party stalwarts when the chairman of the Democrat Central Committee, R. L. Davidson, called on all party members to support Walton's candidacy. Evidently, Davidson announced to the committee that if the members did not support every Democrat running for office in the state, then they should resign. Mrs. Cafky tested the chairman's dictum by resigning her position as vice-chairman. She announced that she would form "clean government clubs" and organize Oklahoma women to fight against the Walton campaign. It was unconscionable to Cafky that women had so little say in the running of the party and that the chairman would support a man with a "long list of crimes against democracy, against society, and against the state."[46] Her purpose, like that of the Klan, was to clean up the Democrat party and rid the party of the ill effects of two years under Walton. The Klan championed a "cleaner" Democrat party, but to them cleaner meant ridding the party of those elements, like the Farmer-Labor Reconstruction League and the Socialists, which divided the party and moved it away from the type of society the Klan envisioned.[47]

There were many in the Democrat party, women in particular, who joined with Klan forces to defeat Governor Walton. It is difficult to say whether women who worked to defeat him were Klanswomen or merely agreed with the Klan that Walton was not fit to represent Oklahoma in the United States Senate. But it is evident that these women viewed politics differently than the old guard who had run the Democrat party machine since before statehood. The women did not believe in following the party line merely for the sake of the party. What mattered more to them was the moral and ethical character of the candidate. Cafky was so strongly opposed to Walton that she led the women in an unprecedented political move when she swung her support to the Klan-endorsed Republican nominee for the U.S. Senate, W. B. Pine from Okmulgee. In order to boost Pine's candidacy among Democrat women, the ladies formed the Pine for Senator Club and adopted the slogan "Beat Walton and vote the rest of the ticket," meaning they only supported Pine, not the Republican ticket.[48]

Klan politics and the autocratic inclinations of Governor Walton made for a volatile political atmosphere in Oklahoma in the mid-1920s. Most women considered that Walton's type of politics was what was generally wrong with state, and that it was their civic responsibility to work toward "clean government." Mrs. Cafky believed that the only way she could work toward better government was not to engage in a political fight with the men of her party. Political infighting was why many women shied away from politics to begin with, and why many women opposed political equality. They feared that suffrage would diminish many of women's most defining characteristics; femininity, gentility, and moral and ethical superiority. The unethical and uncivil nature of politics that Mrs. Cafky tried to avoid was, perhaps, inevitable. Cafky did not have the support of all Democrat women in her stand against Walton. Opposing Cafky and the Democrat women for Pine were other politically prominent women Democrats like Mrs. R. L. Fite, Mrs. Frank Korn, and former state legislator, Mrs. Edith Mitchell. These ladies believed, like the men, that it was better to hold the party together than lose the election because of factionalism.[49] Democrat women were quite outspoken in their views and engaged in heated debates over the Walton issue. The animus of the debate did not go unnoticed by political observers, who were always quick to analyze women's political character. It was especially interesting when women abandoned their ladylike political posture and put on the fighting gloves. As one columnist observed, "To those who want spice in their politics we recommend that they attend future meetings of the Democratic women in this territory. The gentle cut of triple-pointed lampooning, such as was practical in days of yore has been revived. Sweet expletives such as 'shut your mouth' are there slung back and forth with a deftness and abandon that would make old war horses of the campaign platform break down and weep."[50]

The senatorial contest of 1924 had other political repercussions besides alienating some women from the Democrat party. It was also the beginning of the end of the Ku Klux Klan in Oklahoma. In fact, internal strife within the national Klan organization began at the same time that Simmons established the Kamelia, and Evans started the Women of the Ku Klux Klan. The grab for power contest between Simmons and Evans and internal factionalism over lawsuits between the two left many in the membership disillusioned because the principles and integrity of the Klan were somehow lost in the battle.[51] Regardless of the problems experienced by the Klan nationally, in Oklahoma membership held at 100,000 in 1924. The order was also politically strong, winning significant gains in city and state elections. But the political maneuverings by Grand Dragon Jewett in the 1924 senatorial election caused a fissure in the organization that it was never able to bridge.

It all started with the senatorial primary contest in August 1924, when impeached Governor Jack Walton, Klansman and state Representative E. B. Howard, and Tulsa oilman Charles G. Wrightsman vied for the candidacy of their party. Klansmen almost unanimously supported Howard. But when the *Fiery Cross*, the official Klan paper in Oklahoma, supported Wrightsman, Klan membership, believing this to be the official Klan endorsement, followed course and endorsed Wrightsman. On the eve of the primary, however, Grand Dragon Jewett sent a telegram to state locals instructing Klansmen to vote for Howard. By so doing, Jewett successfully split the vote, and Walton won the primary. This was evidently the plan of the Grand Dragon all along. He was a staunch Republican and gambled that if he could split the ticket between Howard and Wrightsman, Walton would win the Democrat nomination, and, in the general election in November, would most surely lose to the Republican candidate, W. B. Pine.[52] Pine won the Senatorial seat. He was a lucky man. Not only did he have the support of the Grand Dragon of the Ku Klux Klan, but also the support of the Democrat women who defected from their party to defeat Walton.

The Oklahoma Klan began its decline after the fall elections, and as 1925 dawned, membership in both the WKKK and the Klan began to wane. As with the men's organization, the WKKK suffered from internal divisions among the leadership. And similarly, lawsuits over WKKK revenues weakened the integrity of the order.[53] The violent nature of the Oklahoma Klan and the publicity generated from this violence also contributed to the decline of the Klan and the WKKK by 1928. In fact, as early as 1923, Klan tactics and violence resulted in a backlash among Oklahoma citizens who joined anti-Klan organizations like the National League of Liberty, National Law and Order League, Local Citizens Club, American Patriots, United Workers, the Farmer-Labor Unions, Loyal Americans, Sons of Valley Forge, Silent Watchmen, Flaming Circle, Royal Blues, and Anti–Ku Klux Klan All American Association. Many of these anti-Klan organizations merged into the Anti–Ku Klux Klan Association, with a membership of 25,000 Oklahomans who represented twenty different organizations in Oklahoma. The Association fought its battle in the Oklahoma legislature by lobbying for a strong anti-Klan bill. Legislators passed the Oklahoma Anti-Mask Law in late 1923, which made it unlawful to where a mask in any attempt to threaten an Oklahoma citizen.[54]

In all, the Women of the Ku Klux Klan organization lasted only five years. Women who joined the Ku Klux Klan were impatient with the slow-grinding wheels of justice. To them, there was a litany of societal problems, including corrupt public officials, cultural decay, and religious contamination, that needed their attention. Many women chose the Klan as the vehicle from which to change society because they could go about their business with little criticism and interference from those who would oppose their actions. The anonymous nature of the Klan does not allow us to investigate as fully as possible women who joined such an ultraconservative organization. It would be interesting to know how many politically active women who were involved in party politics or women's political action groups were also members of the WKKK. Mrs. Cafky denied that she or her husband belonged to the Klan or even agreed with their views. There is no indication that Lola Pearson, vice-chairman of the Republican party and president of the Oklahoma Federation of Women's Clubs belonged to the WKKK. Like many Klanswomen, she was a member of the Order of the Eastern Star, and her husband was one of the founding members of the Masons. Myrtle McDougal, prominent in the Oklahoma Democrat party, also left no record of being a member of the WKKK. *Harlow's Weekly* reported that her husband was a member of the Klan in Creek County. Whether she belonged or not, some people believed that her husband's membership in the Klan cast a negative light on her assuming a leadership role among Democrat women.[55] The Klan was only one organization of many in which conservative women could work to create a better government and a better society. Women also belonged to numerous patriotic organizations in Oklahoma where they kept an ever-vigilant eye on America's worst enemy, communism.

NOTES

1. *Tulsa Daily World*, 28 February 1923.
2. Charles C. Alexander, *The Ku Klux Klan in the Southwest*, (Norman: University of Oklahoma Press, 1995), pp. 14–15; Carter Blue Clark, "A History of the Ku Klux Klan in Oklahoma," (Ph.D. dissertation, 1976), University of Oklahoma, pp. 2–3; See also Leo Kelly, "Black Brush of Hatred KKK on Trial in Altus," *Chronicles of Oklahoma* (Spring 1994); John Higham, *Strangers in the Land: Patterns of American Nativism 1860–1925*, (New Brunswick: Rutgers University Press, 1988).
3. Clark, "The History of the Ku Klux Klan in Oklahoma," pp. 10–11.
4. Clark, "A History of the Ku Klux Klan in Oklahoma," p. 38; *The Kourier Magazine* February 1925.
5. Kathleen M. Blee, *Women of the Klan: Racism and Gender in the 1920s*, (Los Angles: University of California Press, 1991), pp. 13–19.
6. Ibid., p. 13.
7. Clark, "A History of the Ku Klux Klan in Oklahoma," p. 38.
8. Charles C. Alexander, *The Ku Klux Klan in the Southwest*, pp. 1–3; For examples of nomenclature, the national head of organization was the Imperial Wizard. The state leader was the Grand Dragon, the Vice President was the Klaliff, the treasurer was the Klabee and the secretary was the Kligrapp. A district leader was the Great Titan and local chapter leader was the Exalted

Cyclops. Emerson H. Loucks, *Klan in Pennsylvania: A Study in Nativism*, (Harrisburg: The Telegraph Press, 1936), chapter ten.

9. Alexander, *Ku Klux Klan in the Southwest*, pp. 5–9.

10. Clark, "A History of the Ku Klux Klan in Oklahoma," pp. 41–42.

11. Clark, "A History of the Ku Klux Klan in Oklahoma," pp. 41–47.

12. Ibid. p. 22.

13. Clark, "A History of the Ku Klux Klan in Oklahoma," p. 79; Alexander, *The Ku Klux Klan in the Southwest*, p. 79; Laurie Jane Croft, "The Women of the Ku Klux Klan in Oklahoma" (Master's Thesis, University of Oklahoma, 1984), pp. 17–18.

14. Alexander, *The Ku Klux Klan in the Southwest*, p. 100; Clark, "A History of the Ku Klux Klan in Oklahoma," p. 83.

15. *New York Times*, 23 November 1923.

16. Alexander, *The Ku Klux Klan in the Southwest*, p. 103.

17. Kenneth T. Jackson, *The Ku Klux Klan in the City 1915–1930*, (New York: Oxford University Press, 1967), p. 85.

18. *Tulsa Daily World*, 16 February 1923.

19. Alexander, *The Ku Klux Klan in the Southwest*, pps. 30-31; Office of the Imperial Commander Women of the Ku Klux Klan Official Bulletin, April, 1927, Ku Klux Klan Women's Organization, Western History Collection, University of Oklahoma, Norman, Oklahoma. Hereafter cited WKKK.

20. Jackson, *The Ku Klux Klan in The City, 1915-1930*, p. 85.

21. *Tulsa Daily World*, 22 February 1923.

22. *Tulsa Daily World*, 18 April 1923, 20 April 1923, 21 April 1923.

23. Like the Klan, women adopted the same strange nomenclature, overutilizing the letter *K*. For example, the nuts and bolts of WKKK organization can be found in the Kloran (secret work). The songs used at every meeting, the Klonklave, could be found in the Musiklan. Every Klonklave started with the Ku Klux Kreed, officiated by the Excellent Commander, and prayer. led by the Kludd (chaplain). The Klaliff was the president and the Klokard, the lecturer.

24. Croft, "Women in the Ku Klux Klan in Oklahoma," p. 22; Alexander, *The Ku Klux Klan in the Southwest*, p. 102; R. R. Packard to Henry S. Johnson, 22 October 1925, Henry S. Johnson Collection, Western History Collection, University of Oklahoma.

25. *Daily Oklahoman*, 21 September 1947.

26. "The Truth Shall Make You Free," Vertical File, Freemasons, Oklahoma History Society, Oklahoma City.

27. Vertical File, Order of the Eastern Star, Oklahoma Historical Society, Oklahoma City.

28. Membership cards, WKKK.

29. Victor E. Harlow, *Makers of Government in Oklahoma*, (Oklahoma City: Harlow Publishing Company, 1930), p. 117. The Hudson Collection at the Oklahoma Historical Society in Oklahoma City has the membership list of the ladies who belonged to the Coalgate Klan in 1924. From this list of names, it was possible to locate biographical information on several women, which helped to provide a clearer picture of women in the Klan organization. In contrast, the Organization of the Women of the Ku Klux Klan Collection at the Western History Archive at the University of Oklahoma has a stamp of censorship on the collection, prohibiting researchers from viewing the names of the ladies in the Cherokee Klan. This is sensitive material for an institution whose vice-president in 1923 held a leadership position in the Oklahoma state organization of the Ku Klux Klan.

30. "A Patriotic Call" WKKK; Croft, "The Women of the Ku Klux Klan in Oklahoma," p. 25.

31. Croft, "The Women of the Ku Klux Klan in Oklahoma," p. 35.

32. Ibid. p. 29.

33. Blee, *Women of the Klan: Racism and Gender in the 1920s*, p. 36.

34. *Kourier Magazine*, August 1925, September 1927, Carter Blue Clark Collection, Western History Collections, University of Oklahoma. Hereafter cited CBC.

35. Ibid.

36. The *Imperial Night-Hawk*, 15 October 1924, CBC.

37. *Kourier Magazine*, September 1927, CBC.

38. The *Fish Hook*, 14 July 1923, Henry S. Johnson Collection, Western History Collection, University of Oklahoma.

39. Unidentified newspaper article, Henry S. Johnson Collection, Western History Collection, University of Oklahoma; Kathleen Blee also suggests that the charitable activities of Klanswomen served to cast the Ku Klux Klan as less racist, less violent, and more humanitarian. Kathleen M. Blee, "Women in the 1920s' Ku Klux Klan Movement," *Feminist Studies* 17, no. 1 (Spring 1991): 57.

40. Bulletin, Office of the Commander Women of the Ku Klux Klan, April 1927, February 1928, Ku Klux Klan Women's Organization, WKKK.

41. Clark, "The History of the Ku Klux Klan in Oklahoma," pp. 169–177; Danny Goble, *Oklahoma Politics: A History*, (Norman: University of Oklahoma Press, 1982), p. 132.

42. Interview, Leon Hirsh, 25 April 1974, CBC.

43. As mentioned in chapter four, the October special election was originally called by Walton for the purpose of placing before Oklahoma voters five amendments to the state constitution. One of them was the women's amend-

ment, which, if passed, would give Oklahoma women the right to run for state office.

44. Clark, "The History of the Ku Klux Klan in Oklahoma," pp. 181–196.

45. Cafky was born in Verden, Illinois, on July 19, 1870. She attended Woman's College in Jacksonville, Illinois. She was the mother of four children, and although she considered herself a homemaker as a profession, she was a regent of the University Prepatory School and Jr. College in Tonkawa and Auto Tax Collector for Beaver County. She moved to Oklahoma in 1895 and lived in Woodward, Weatherford, and Elk City before she and her husband, O. H. Cafky, settled in Forgan. Rex F. Harlow, *Makers of Government in Oklahoma*, (Oklahoma City: Harlow Publishing Company, 1930), p. 17.

46. *Harlow's Weekly*, 3 October 1924.

47. *Oklahoma Fiery Cross*, 12 November 1924, Campbell Russell Collection, Western History Collection, University of Oklahoma.

48. *Harlow's Weekly*, 27 September 1924.

49. Ibid.

50. *Harlow's Weekly*, 20 September 1924.

51. Clark, "History of the Ku Klux Klan in Oklahoma," p. 224.

52. *Harlow's Weekly*, 9 August 1924; Alexander, *The Ku KluxKlan in the Southwest*, pp. 200–202.

53. Ibid., p. 230.

54. Ibid., pp. 221–223.

55. *Harlow's Weekly*, 6 September 1924.

At the Far Right
of the Political Spectrum
Americanism vs. Communism

In 1931 Lola Clark Pearson, chairman of the Americanization Committee of the National General Federation of Women's Clubs, wrote to federation members throughout the country inquiring about subversive political activities in their communities. Pearson believed that such information was pertinent to the future direction of the General Federation's Americanization programs. She explained in her letter to state club women that "I am thinking of all movements which sponsor disorderly demonstrations, opposition to our form of government, or change by force." She identified these movements under several banners, such as "Communism," "Sovietism," "Red Menace," or "Third International."[1] It was characteristic of Pearson to be concerned with the spread of political ideas that threatened democracy and the structure of capitalism. Pearson was a political conservative from Oklahoma who believed that those who embraced Socialist ideals intended to destroy the traditions, customs, and institutions of the American people. Lola Pearson countered the spread of socialism by educating newly enfranchised Oklahoma women to distinguish between the rhetoric of political activists who sought solutions to societal ills by expanding the power of the state, and that of those who believed in individual initiative to solve community problems. Pearson also lectured women about the United States' involvement in world affairs. She spoke out against foreign policy that threatened American sovereignty and against international economic agreements that weakened capitalism.

Lola Pearson was representative of many politically active conservative women in the 1920s who believed that in the wake of the Communist takeover in Russia in 1917, it was prudent to safeguard American democracy and capitalism. But Pearson was not a reactionary who painted those who held different philosophical ideals about government and society with the same red brush. She was a careful researcher who compiled most of her information from primary sources, including Communist publications. She then incorporated this material into her speeches as evidence of radical subversion of American institutions. From the sources she gathered on radical activities in the United States, it is possible to illustrate the Communist program that seemed so threatening to conservatives, and the political backlash, which moved the ideology of many Oklahoma women further to the right on the political spectrum.

As a conservative, Lola Pearson worked to implement reform and good government through her club work and political party activities. As already mentioned, Pearson was one of two women the Republican party chose as delegates to attend the 1920 Republican National Convention. And in 1922 the Republican party chose her to be vice-chairman of the state Republican party.[2] Pearson was typical of many women who became involved in party politics in the 1920s, in that she was middle class, was well educated, was employed in a professional capacity, and championed many issues and causes that club women fought for in the late-nine-teenth and early-twentieth centuries.[3] Lola Clark was born near Elwood, Iowa, in 1871. After attending Cornell and Morningside Colleges, she taught school in Iowa until her marriage to John C. Pearson in 1899. The Pearsons lived in Pierson, Iowa, where John served as mayor from 1898 until 1905. The couple moved to Marshall, Oklahoma, in 1905 to enter into several business ventures ranging from owning grain elevators to investment in coal, lumber and real estate. The Pearsons were promi-nent members of the Marshall community. John served as mayor for two terms, and both were active members of the Methodist Episcopal Church and initial members of the Fraternal Order of the Masons and the Order of the Eastern Star.[4] Lola Pearson first became involved in club work in Oklahoma when she organized the Marshall Woman's Club. In 1921 the membership of the Oklahoma General Federation of Women's Clubs elected Pearson state director. In 1920 the national organization asked her to chair the Americanization committee, which she did until 1935.[5] Along with her club work, Pearson influenced women through her posi-tion as home editor of the *Oklahoma Farmer*, and later as associate editor of the *Farmer Stockman*.

During the 1920 presidential campaign, Pearson was one of the Republican speakers who joined state and national leaders in a lecture touring troupe dubbed the Flying Squadron. Her speeches to those gath-ered at political rallies addressed the merits of the Republican program and offered advice to women about their new responsibilities as voters. Pearson told her audiences that "suffrage was a great privilege and a great responsibility," and that there was, "no nation greater than its women."[6] But she warned women to be wary of politicians who spread propaganda and subversive ideals that, in her words, "creep in the guise of personal liberty." She called on women to have "eternal vigilance" and, most of all, to "preserve American institutions."[7] The threat of subversion of the American system seemed even more acute after the first World War and the Russian Revolution. It was alarming to conservatives that most eastern European immigrants did not speak English and knew little about America's political or social culture. It concerned Lola Pearson that only one out of five immigrant women could speak or read English, and that out of more than a million immigrant women, only thirteen thousand had any schooling. In a message to club women, Pearson wrote that "illiteracy furnishes fertile ground for the development of anarchy…bolshevism and discontent sowed by active enemy alien agents."[8] She believed that Americanization programs were important if immigrant people were to become patriotic Americans, and she looked to Oklahoma's club women to play a central role in educating immigrant women to embrace traditional American values. Pearson suggested that Federated Club women seek out and show immigrant women the guiding virtues of the American home. This association also would benefit club women as well. Pearson surmised that "we need personal contact with [immigrant women] to develop the broad mindedness that begets understanding."[9]

If immigrant women understood the principles of democracy and the benefits of capitalism, then they would educate their children to become responsible American citizens. But club women had to be ever vigilant to the insidious methods used by the radicals, who sought to capture the minds of young children. Minnie J. Nielson, State Superintendent of Public Instruction in South Dakota, warned Oklahoma women that they must vote in the November 1922 election to defeat candidates who represented the farmers. From her experience in South Dakota, the Non-Partisan League used farmers' programs to "spread through the schools and libraries the doctrines of Socialism, Bolshevism, and Free Love."[10] The Farmer-Labor Reconstruction League in Oklahoma was similar to South Dakota's Non-Partisan League. The Oklahoma league filled the void left by the defunct Socialist party in addressing the economic concerns of the farmers in the post–World War I economic decline. And many of the veteran Socialist leaders, like Oscar Ameringer and Patrick Nagle, influenced the League's party platform in 1921, which resounded many of the Socialist ideals of the previous decade.[11] There were other signs that Socialists were trying to revitalize their political activity in Oklahoma. As early as 1918, some Socialists believed that the decision of the party to officially oppose America's involvement in the European war was a mistake. H. H. Stallard, billed as "an Oklahoma Socialist lecturer," suggested that the party "repudiate" its stand on the war. He called on chairmen of Socialist locals to poll their membership on the war issue and strongly suggested that they vote to support the United States government. He argued that when the first vote was taken, they did not realize the threat of Germany to Europe, especially Russia. Their initial concern was a war created by Imperialism that took the focus off of building an "industrial democracy by capturing the political power." This goal became impossible when the party all but disintegrated during the federal government's patriotic campaign to rally support for the war. However, Socialists could easily change their position on the war by using the German threat to Russia. In this way, the party could regain prestige as a viable political party in the country.[12] At the same time that Stallard was trying to return the party to its former self, Victor Berger, Socialist leader and editor of the Socialist paper the *Milwaukee Leader*, was in Oklahoma to assist in arranging facilities for a new Socialist paper, the *Oklahoma Leader*.[13]

By 1923 there was little evidence that the Socialist party was going to regain strength in the state. Those who once worked to build the party in the early part of the century put their efforts behind the Reconstruction League and the Democrat party. But there seemed to be a cautious vigilance by many who believed that the Socialists would continue to insinuate their ideals into the American system. Governor Walton reaffirmed this belief when he appointed Mrs. Patrick S. Nagle to the State Board of Public Affairs in 1923.[14] Critics shouted that the appointment was payback to Socialist leader Pat Nagle for his advisory position in Walton's campaign for governor, and that Mrs. Nagle was a "Red Card Socialist." J. W. Kayser, editor of the *Oklahoma Star*, who held the position on the board previous to the appointment of Mrs. Nagle, exclaimed, "Not in our wildest flights of fancy did we dream that the wife of Pat Nagle would be given the best position at the hands of a governor elected on the Democratic ticket." To many, Mrs. Nagle's new position was an open invitation for further appointments of Socialists to government positions.[15]

While it appeared that there was little Socialist activity in the state, Lola Pearson gathered proof to the contrary. Mrs. Randolph Frothingham, secretary and treasurer of the *Woman Patriot*, sent Pearson sufficient evidence of Communist intent to subvert American culture. The *Woman Patriot* played an important role in advising conservative women about the motives and goals of those on the left.[16] For example, the newspaper informed conservative women of the Communist plan to provide government assistance to the schoolchildren of workers and poor farmers. Several of Mrs. Frothingham's sources were of interest to Pearson and other conservatives because the material illustrated the Communist goal to incorporate American children into the class struggle to defeat capitalism. In the "Bulletin for Teachers of Communist Children's Sections," Pearson learned that the Communists believed the most exciting part of their plan was the Communist Children's Movement. Evidently, American schoolchildren were the new target and recruitment activity moved to the "nuclei in the bourgeois school." The booklet described that the educational plan would provide a "Leninist" approach to learning that would first teach the "education toward Leninism" and then advance to Leninist theory. "Leninist education makes proletarians realize the conditions under which they live. It explains to them what social life in its various aspects really is. This education paves the way for Leninist theory."[17]

Changing the capitalist system by building a strong organization of young Communists was not entirely directed at urban areas where there was more of a concentration of working-class families, but at the rural regions of the country like Oklahoma. Their slogan was "Capture the Village." In small towns and "villages" the Communists recognized that the "bourgeois" had quite a bit of influence over "proletarian" children, especially through such organizations as the Red Cross, Boy Scouts, and "Fascist" sports programs.[18] It was, therefore, vital to counter bourgeois organizations with Communist youth clubs like the Young Pioneers. The Communists initially organized the Young Pioneers, the children's branch of the Young Communist League, to provide activities more in line with Socialist doctrine and Communist activities. It was important for Communists to educate working-class children about injustices that they believed existed in American society. They especially taught children to organize against the United States military war preparedness program. In this endeavor, the target was the Boy Scouts of America, an organization they believed posed as a para-military boot camp for young boys. An article in Lola Pearson's the *Young Comrade* explained how large congressional appropriations to the War Department and Navy were indications that America was preparing for war—a war that would only benefit the capitalist class. One way in which the children could fight against capitalist wars was to wage war against the Boy Scouts of America. The magazine advocated that it was "the duty of every child of the working class to fight against the Boy Scouts."[19]

Whether in rural or urban areas, Communist youth organizations were important in converting American youth into faithful Communists. The *Young Pioneer* magazine, dubbed "a paper for workers' and farmers' children," and the official magazine of the Young Pioneers, instructed children about the evils of a capitalist society and how the authorities, such as school officials, sought to control the Communist protest against societal wrongs. One article in the *Young Pioneer* illustrated the poor condition of public schools attended by workers' children in New York City. The school's classrooms were overcrowded, the cafeteria served poor-quality food, and there was no bus service, which forced many children to walk long distances to school in bad weather. The magazine editor pointed out that any protest of these unsuitable conditions was met with a "campaign of terror" and urged the children of New York to "answer the attack by mass protest and demonstrations. We must force the servant principal and the teachers to allow workers' children to show their solidarity with the working class." This was also the message of Communists in Milwaukee. When school officials threatened to expel the children if they organized a Young Pioneers club, the Communists encouraged them to stage a mass protest.[20] The Communist call for resistance was realized in Cleveland, Ohio, when the Young Pioneers held a mass demonstration to end car fares in the city. It is not clear if the protest failed or not, but the authorities jailed the young demonstrators.[21]

In addition to the apparent threat of Communism to American children, many conservatives believed that feminists, in concert with the left, were trying to undermine the structure of the family through the legislative process. In 1925 women at the federal Children's Bureau proposed to Congress a Child Labor Amendment to the constitution. Besides the Sheppard-Towner Act, there was no other measure in the 1920s that more brought out the ire of conservative women and helped ignite conservative activism. Several salient factors shaped the conservative argument against a national amendment on child labor. First, the Child Labor Amendment originated with Socialist Florence Kelly and the National Child Labor Committee. Kelly was well known in conservative circles for her lobbying efforts to convince Congress to pass the Sheppard-Towner Act. Her association with the Child Labor Amendment was, therefore, suspect. Conservatives also warned of the association of the Children's Bureau with Socialist activists like Alexandra Kollontai and Anna Louise Strong. Kollontai was a Bolshevik revolutionary who swept into power with Lenin in the Russian Revolution of 1917. In the formation of the Bolshevik government, Lenin appointed Kollontai as director of the Bolshevik Department of Public Welfare.[22] She was also the first director of the Children's Colonization Movement in Russia. Kollontai held some very revolutionary ideas about the role of women and children in a Socialist state. To Kollontai, the bourgeois marriage was outdated. A better system would be "free union of men and women who are lovers and comrades." And, regarding the fate of children, Kollontai continued, "The worker mother who is conscious of her social function will rise to a point where she no longer differentiates between yours and mine; she must remember that there are henceforth only our children, those of the Communist state, the common possession of all workers."[23] During her tenure as director of public welfare in Russia, Kollontai wrote several books on the welfare of women and children. She was also a leading source for the Children's Bureau publications in the United States on maternity and infant care. The political conservative could easily conceive that there was a threat to American democratic institutions by political activists like Kollontai. Also of concern was that her philosophy on the role of women and children in the family was regarded so highly by the women at the Children's Bureau, themselves adherents of Socialist political philosophy.

The association of Anna Louise Strong with the Children's Bureau and Russian Children's Colonization Movement was also of great concern to conservatives. Strong was an exhibit expert employed by the Children's Bureau and the author of bureau publications. In March 1925, with the funding from American sympathizers, Strong began work on a children's colony in Russia. The Soviet government supported Strong's colonization efforts by giving her 900 acres, which included the buildings of an old monastery, plus the properties of the abandoned homes of dukes, monks, and sympathizers of the Czar. The children's colonies were centers where Russian children were housed and "educated to be future leaders in the government and development of Russia."[24]

Hearings held before the Committee on the Judiciary in February and March of 1924 clearly outlined the differing opinions held by conservative and progressive women on the Child Labor Amendment. Over all, women's organizations favored the amendment, but for different reasons.

It appeared that the basic reason many supported the amendment was that, even though most states had child labor laws, the laws were either not enforced or did not go far enough in prohibiting child labor. Mary Stewart, chairman of the Women's Committee for the Amendment, represented such organizations as the Young Women's Christian Association and the General Federation of Women's Clubs. Stewart testified that women she represented believed that the amendment would empower Congress to pass legislation to enforce restrictions on child labor, but the amendment would also preserve the right of states to pass laws to the same effect.[25] Women in the Republican party also supported the federal amendment. Mrs. Harriet Taylor Upton, of the National Executive Committee of the Republican party, favored the amendment because there did not seem to be any other solution to the child labor problem. She testified that Republican women were "not in favor of paternal government; we would not care for that if we could do this in any other way."[26] Mrs. Emily Newell Blair, vice-chairman of the National Democrat Committee, echoed Upton's sentiments. But, the real opposition came from women who made the connection between those who championed federal protection of American children and the Socialist ideal of state organization of children. Mary G. Kilbrith, president of the Woman's Patriot Publishing Company, was the most outspoken critic of the amendment. She testified that her initial reason for opposing the amendment was that it violated states' rights and would create unnecessary bureaucracy. She viewed this as a threat to liberty and quoted the colonial complaint against King George III: "He has erected a multitude of new offices, and sent hither swarms of officers to harass our people and eat out their substance." Her second argument was that by denying children the right to experience work, the country would be creating a generation of people who did not know how to work; they would not know the value of a work ethic. Kilbrith explained that "the boy or girl who arrives at the age of 18 having had no work training has lost the most valuable years of his or her life." Kilbrith's most ardent argument was that those who authored the legislation from the Children's Bureau were using the amendment to gain authority over American youth. Her evidence was from a speech given by Grace Abbott, head of the Children's Bureau, to the Socialist organization, the National Women's Trade Union League of America. In her speech, Abbott suggested to her audience that they had the opportunity to include in the amendment "language giving us constitutional authority to do some of the other things in the federal field that we might like to do." Kilbrith also pointed out that Florence Kelly, chief architect of the amendment, was duly aligned with the Socialists. She was a translator of Marx and Engels and the editor of a Socialist paper in Germany.[27]

Mary Kilbrith and the editors of the *Woman Patriot* fought against the Child Labor Amendment because they believed that feminists wanted to nationalize children. It was, therefore, the conservatives' responsibility to alert Americans to the association of Communist Alexandra Kollontai and Anna Louise Strong with the Children's Bureau and bureau legislation. To prove their thesis, the editors of the *Woman Patriot* printed numerous articles of the Communist intent to weaken traditional American family values. The editors' method of convincing the readership was to reprint parts of propaganda from Communist newspapers like the *Daily Worker*. In this way, the information presented to conservative women was accurate, but generalizations made about the goals of the Communists were misleading and tended to generate anxiety among conservative women about the nature and goals of the Communist movement. For example, the *Daily Worker* informed its readers that they must convince state legislatures to pass the Child Labor Amendment and to add "a law providing full government maintenance of all schoolchildren of workers and poor farmers." The *Woman Patriot* reported this but added the "Nationalization of Children Now Openly Avowed As Real Object" of the Communist.[28] It is not clear whether the women at the Children's Bureau had ulterior motives for promoting the Child Labor Amendment. Historical studies of the bureau point out that the primary goal was to protect childhood, and basically, the bureau supported middle-class family values. Women employed at the Children's Bureau believed the ideal family consisted of two parents, where fathers worked and mothers took care of the home.[29]

The United States Congress passed the Child Labor Amendment in 1925. The amendment, however, was not ratified by the states. One reason for its failure was that most states already had child labor laws that protected children in industry. Oklahoma's child labor laws, along with the compulsory attendance law, went into effect June 11, 1909.[30] There is little evidence that there was a lot of support in Oklahoma for what feminists hoped would be the twentieth amendment to the federal constitution. The amendment passed the committee on constitutional amendments in January 1925. But since there was "much opposition to this amendment," political observers accurately predicted that it would not pass in the state legislature.[31]

Another sign of the ideological separation between women on the right and the left of the political spectrum began as early as 1923, when new conservative organizations such as the Sentinels of the Republic and traditional patriotic groups such as the Daughters of the American Revolution (DAR) and the Women's Auxiliary of the American Legion, grew in membership. The Sentinels of the Republic began when prominent politicians gathered at the New York City home of Charles S. Fairchild, secretary of the treasury for President Grover Cleveland. Their idea was to create a patriotic organization similar to that of Samuel Adams in early America. Many considered him the historical founder of the Sentinels of the Republic. They believed that the organization would serve as an informational clearinghouse for patriots. In particular, the Sentinels vowed "to maintain the fundamental principles of the American Constitution, to oppose further federal encroachment upon the reserved rights of the states, to stop the growth of socialism and to prevent the concentration of power in Washington." By so doing, the Sentinels stood against the Child Labor Amendment. They viewed it as "a violation of the principle of local self-government." When the amendment went down to defeat, the Sentinels claimed credit. By 1923, the Sentinels of the Republic had branches of their organization in 43 states and 480 cities and towns. It is difficult to estimate how many Oklahoma women belonged, but it is known that Oklahoma conservative, Alice Robertson, was a member of the Committee of Correspondence.[32]

In Oklahoma and nationwide, membership in other conservative organizations like the DAR and Women's Auxiliary increased by the mid 1920s. The most apparent reason was that conservative women were reacting (and for some, overreacting) to the spread of Communism; they fought back by promoting patriotic organizations who supported the United States military's preparedness programs. The DAR in particular reflected the conservative move to the right. Up to the 1920s, the DAR promoted progressive concerns like conservation, vocational education, children's playgrounds, and the Children's Bureau in the federal government.[33] By the early 1920s, the leadership moved the organization into the conservative column with their stand that the country needed to maintain a strong military to protect the United States from foreign influence. DAR membership in Oklahoma included many women who were influential in Oklahoma politics. Anna Korn, active member of the Democrat party and the Women's Legislative Council, was an organizer and regent for the DAR in her community and a member of the United

States Daughters of the War of 1812.[34] Alice Robertson was regent of the Anyastee chapter of the DAR and, although it is not mentioned in Lola Pearson's biographical sources that she was a member of the DAR, she subscribed to the DAR magazine.

The DAR magazine was very similar to the *Woman Patriot* in that many of the articles focused on a perceived Communist threat to the country. To counter subversive activities in the United States, DAR leaders recommended that women take a more aggressive stand in promoting a strong national defense program. The magazines' major stories throughout 1927 concerned the activities of the DAR's Department of National Defense Committee. Of note was the participation of women in The Women's Patriotic Conference on National Defense. More than twenty-seven women's organizations attended the conference in Washington, D.C., in February 1927 to discuss many aspects of national defense. One particular point seemed critical: that the United States maintain a strong military. The reasoning was that in the past the country was unprepared for war, and this cost too much in lives and money. The women concluded that with an adequate national defense program, America's future peace and welfare would be assured. Conference leaders called on women to support the National Defense Act of 1920 and ROTC programs on college campuses. It was also important that women oppose radicals who conservatives believed were infiltrating schools and colleges with the intent to convince students to resist the military, and that women investigate whether college curricula were patriotic.[35]

Another theme prevalent in the DAR magazine was the threat of Communism to the American family. What the editors of the magazine warned against, Lola Pearson must have already discovered in her reading of the Communist youth magazine, the *Young Pioneer*. Editorials reinforced the conservative theory that Communism targeted American children and also associated the writings of Alexandra Kollantai to the undermining of American family values. By 1927, Kollantai was Russia's ambassador to Mexico. In her pamphlet, "Communism and the Family," she wrote that the traditional family was disintegrating and that "our new man in our new society is to be molded by Socialist organizations like playgrounds, gardens, homes, and many other such institutions, in which a child will pass the greater part of a day, and where intelligent educators make of him a Communist."[36]

The Women's American Legion Auxiliary also gained in membership in Oklahoma throughout the 1920s. The Legion Auxiliary initially worked to provide support for the American Legion but turned into a women's patriotic organization whose main goal was to combat un-American activities in the country. Similar to Lola Pearson's work on the Americanization committee of the GFWC, women in the Auxiliary focused attacks against radical subversion of American values by working to eliminate illiteracy and to educate the foreign born. Mrs. Brown, speaking before the Auxiliary convention in Lawton in 1923, informed her audience that "We must fight the insidious foe of illiteracy with every weapon at our command, cooperating with schools, women's clubs, and other progressive organizations, for to be denied the right to knowledge is tragedy." The message was consistent with other conservative organizations; education was an important tool in fighting the spread of political ideologies that undermined the American ideal of government and society. The Auxiliary worked with the Bureau of Naturalization in organizing citizenship classes to teach the "rights and obligations of an American citizen." Auxiliary women were also concerned about the Communist youth movement, which they viewed as "the best section of the Communist Internationale." The women believed that it was essential to support the work of the Boy Scouts and Campfire Girls by offering supervision and leadership.[37] The Legion Auxiliary also encouraged the members to "report any anti-American propaganda in our histories or other text books.... It is the patriotic duty to protect our youth against the poison of Sovietism, Communism, or extreme radicalism."[38]

Auxiliary members understood that the Communists sought to indoctrinate newly enfranchised women by appealing to their sensibilities about world peace. As one Auxiliary report concluded, "what could be more subtle and more insidious than to approach women with an outcry against war and an appeal for the disarmament of the nation in the sacred name of peace?" To prove their contentions that Socialists used women to further their cause, auxiliary leaders pointed to the history of socialism. The principles of socialism as espoused in 1927 were very similar to a Socialist cult called the Society of Illuminati, an organization formed in Bavaria in 1776 by Adam Weishaupt. Basically, Weishaupt called for the destruction of all government, of patriotism, of property rights, of the right of inheritance, of religion, and of the family. To do this, Weishaupt believed women were the best weapon. The Woman's Auxiliary quoted Weishaupt as saying, "Through women we may often work the best in this world. To insinuate ourselves with them, to win their confidence ... should be one of our cleverest studies, for they are easily led."[39]

The evidence of possible radical subversion of the American life was so overwhelming to conservatives that by mid-decade they were fighting back in a most novel manner—with the aid of the United States War Department. A publication held by Lola Pearson called the *Spider Web Chart* was compiled by the War Department and claimed to connect women who worked for international peace with Socialist organizations. The *Spider Web Chart* was the War Department's response to initiatives by women's peace organizations to curtail military spending and abolish the Defense Act of 1920. Women concerned about international peace first organized the Women's Peace Party in 1915. This organization grew into the Women's International League for Peace and Freedom (WILPF) by 1920. The WILPF encouraged women to become politically active in formulating foreign policy. In the 1920s, the members of the WILPF directed their campaign for peace at the War Department. As a result, the War Department and the WILPF declared war on one another over their respective convictions on the welfare of Americans. The women in the WILPF believed that federal spending should be for societal ills at home and not to prepare America for international conflict. The War Department, on the other hand, believed that those who advocated a weak military program left America defenseless against "numerous organized groups in our body politic striving for class or sectional advantage; absurd political beliefs oftentimes striking at the very foundation of our form of government."[40] In particular, the War Department considered that the Defense Act of 1920 should be stronger, or the country could suffer from a lack of funding for military preparedness. The ladies of the WILPF fought to have the Defense Act discontinued altogether. Personnel at the War Department sent the *Spider Web Chart* out to organizations and conservative newspapers across the country in May 1923. The chart connected feminists to radical associations in the country, which further proved to conservative women that feminists were aligned with socialism and Communist activity.

There is no evidence that Oklahoma women formed organizations solely to work for world peace in the 1920s. The unpopular League of Women Voters, however, brought into the state women speakers who were connected with international peace organizations. In June of 1923, members of the LWV invited Mrs. Lewis Rose of Hartford, Connecticut, to speak at the league conference in Okmulgee. Rose spent the winter of 1921–22 in Europe studying postwar political and economic conditions and, on her return to the United States, embarked on a speaking tour under the auspices of the International Cooperation to Prevent War. Mrs. Rose was evidently a draw card played by state organizers of the LWV to help launch a branch of the league in Okmulgee.[41]

In 1931, when Lola Pearson wrote to women in the General Federation of Women's Clubs throughout the United States seeking information about Communist activities in their communities, the country was facing difficult economic problems and rising unemployment. Historically it was during economic recessions that socialism appealed to those on the bottom rung of the prosperity ladder. The worsening economic depression of the 1930s, therefore, opened the door for Communists to win converts to their cause. Many of the replies to Pearson's query reflected the growing radicalism by Communist agitators who were openly protesting the adverse economic condition of the country. In Washington state clubwomen believed that Communists localized their recruitment to the Finnish farming and fishing communities where the economy was unstable. Mable Campbell allowed that the "hard times" were just making it to the Pacific Northwest, and Communist propaganda, spread through Finnish newspapers, was starting to appeal to those who were experiencing the economic difficulties.[42] Alice Yeakel of the Indiana Federation of Women's Clubs also found a correlation between unemployment and Communist activity in her state. The clubwoman thought it important that men find employment because "the man or woman without a job is naturally more fertile soil for this pernicious doctrine than one who has an assured income."[43] In Utah women came to the same conclusion that radicalism was most likely to be found among a high concentration of workers either unemployed or facing layoffs. Mrs. G. Falck of Ogden, Utah, wrote Pearson that Communist groups in her state were affiliated with the labor unions. But she also informed Pearson that the cell of Communist activity was in Salt Lake City, where Falck maintained the mayor was a Communist sympathizer and allowed "Reds" to hold their meetings in City Hall.[44]

The report to Pearson from clubwomen in Minnesota confirmed what many conservative women came to believe about Communist activity in the country in the 1920s. Mary LaRue from the Minnesota Federation of Women's Clubs was very alarmed with Communist activity in her state and the "insidious operators in women's clubs, churches, and other organizations." She was especially upset by the progress of the Communist Youth Movement and its planned disruption in public schools. She reported to Pearson that "parades of little folk carried banners denouncing our flag, our schools, and employers in vilest terms with crude illustrations." Communist activity was so intense that mob violence was becoming more and more prevalent. She related that men from the Union Mission broke into a grocery and meat store across from the women's clubhouse. What seemed to bother LaRue the most was that after the authorities arrested the men, meal tickets for dinner at the mission were found in their pockets. In defense for their actions, the men stated that they were not stealing but that they were entitled to the food. The women's response in Minnesota was to organize patriotic women to fight against Communism. LaRue and other "sane women" formed an auxiliary to the American Coalition Society, a group dedicated to researching radicalism in all countries.[45] Like Minnesota, Wisconsin had considerable Communist activity, which was perhaps not unexpected in a state with a history of socialism and a strong Socialist party. Theodora Youmans reported that there were Communist camps throughout the state, and students in the Communist youth organizations demonstrated in the public schools.[46] Communism was evidently so prevalent in Wisconsin that Helen K. Stuart, federation officer from the sixth district in Oshkosh, scolded Pearson and the National Organization of Federated Clubs for not being more aware of the radicalism and having no program in place to educate clubwomen. In a rather curt letter to Pearson, Stuart advised that "the most important question before our nation today" is Communism.[47] The response from clubwomen in South Carolina was different than in the more industrial regions of the North, where many industrial workers came from counties sympathetic to socialism. Mrs. Patterson of the South Carolina Federation of Women's Clubs informed Pearson that Communist activity in her state was not out in the open. She explained that door-to-door salesmen sold books that were purported to be Bible stories. Patterson bought a set to investigate what other women had reported about the books. She found that "the first volume appeared religious, the second less—with a vein of skepticism, and they became more so until they ended with an attack—malicious and bitter—upon the government of the United States and all religions."[48]

As Communist activities continued to accelerate in the states, clubwomen stepped up their efforts to combat the spread by joining patriotic organizations like the DAR. Ethel White of the Rhode Island State Federation of Women's Clubs informed Pearson that there were five "Communistic" headquarters in Rhode Island. White maintained that the DAR and other patriotic societies were "very active and interested" in the problem and that "everything is being done in the state that is possible."

The women organized the Rhode Island Women's Patriotic Conference on National Defense, where they invited university professors to lecture on Communist activities in the United States and Russia.[49]

In Oklahoma, Pearson learned of Communist agitation in the state from clubwomen in southern Oklahoma. After receiving Pearson's letter, Julie Floyd of Duncan talked to several people in her community and in Lawton. Both the county attorney and a representative from the Salvation Army informed Floyd that there were strangers in their community, "agitators," working among the farmers who were experiencing economic difficulties. The radicals threatened that, if things did not change, there would be food riots. The men circulated literature, handbills, and subscriptions to the Socialist paper, the *United Farmer,* and lectured the people that "only by your fight against Capitalism, in alliance with the workers, can the farmer free himself from oppression." Authorities found the situation so threatening in Lawton that they asked the commander at Fort Sill to send artillerymen to put down any rioting, and the sheriff deputized American Legionaries for special riot control duty. But all was for naught. As Julia Floyd admitted to Pearson, "The riot did not come off."[50]

What clubwomen feared in the prosperity of the 1920s became more of a reality in the economic depression ushered in by the stock market crash of 1929. Many people began to doubt whether an economy based on competition and the free market system could meet the needs of all the people. The ideal of a cooperative commonwealth espoused by Socialists in the early twentieth century was once again promoted to Oklahomans as a better and fairer economic way of life. The depression also opened the door for greater government involvement in the American system. What conservatives fought for most in the 1920s was an unbridled economy and less government regulation. Especially important was to guard against a paternalistic government that conservatives believed would infringe on American liberty. With the election of Franklin D. Roosevelt to the United States presidency in 1932 and the implementation of his economic and social programs as outlined in his New Deal, conservatism no longer dominated political ideology. As the country moved to the left on the political spectrum, Americans tried to cope with the possible collapse of cherished American institutions. Most Oklahoma women in the 1930s, like many across the country, were more inclined toward working for social uplift than changing societal problems through women's political activities.

NOTES

1. Letter, 6 April 1931, Lola Clark Pearson Collection, Western History Collection, University of Oklahoma, Norman, Oklahoma. Hereafter cited LCP.

2. F. D. Bearly to Lola Clark Pearson, 17 March 1922, LCP.

3. Sophonisba P. Breckinridge, *Women in the Twentieth Century, A Study of Their Political, Social, and Economic Activities*, (New York: McGraw-Hill, 1933), p. 326; Kristi Anderson, *After Suffrage Women in Partisan and Electoral Politics before the New Deal*, (Chicago: The University of Chicago Press, 1996), pp. 104, 137.

4. Inventory to John Cannon Pearson Collection, Western History Collection, University of Oklahoma, Norman, Oklahoma.

5. Biographical file, LCP.

6. Lola Clark Pearson, speech notes, (no title), LCP.

7. Lola Clark Pearson, speech notes, "Our Responsibilities," LCP.

8. Lola Clark Pearson, "America's Greatest Problem," LCP.

9. Lola Clark Pearson, "Americans All," LCP.

10. Minnie J. Nielson, "A Message to Oklahoma Womanhood," 1922, LCP.

11. Danny Goble, *Oklahoma Politics*, (Norman: University of Oklahoma Press, 1982), p. 112; James R. Green, *Grass-Roots Socialism Radical Movements in the Southwest 1895–1943*, (Baton Rouge: Louisiana State University Press, 1978), p. 398.

12. *Harlow's Weekly*, 22 May 1918.

13. *Harlow's Weekly*, 24 April 1918.

14. Mrs. Nagle was born in Franklin, Pennsylvania, and moved to Oklahoma in 1889. After attending college in Kansas, she married Patrick Sarsfield Nagle. The couple had two children. Mrs. Nagle's brother was W. A. McCartney, a member of the First and Second Territorial Senates. The Nagles worked for the Socialist cause in Oklahoma and worked together in the Walton campaign. Victor Harlow, *Makers of Oklahoma Government*, (Oklahoma City: Oklahoma Publishing Comp., 1930), p. 559.

15. *Harlow's Weekly*, 20 January 1923, 27 January 1923.

16. The *Woman Patriot* was the former antisuffrage newspaper, the *Woman's Protest*. The *Woman Citizen* was the suffrage counterpart.

17. *Bulletin for Teachers of Communist Children's Sections*, (London: Publishing House of the Young Communist International, 1925), LCP.

18. Ibid.

19. It should be noted that Lola Pearson marked the part of the magazine that referenced the Boy Scouts of America, the *Young Comrade* July 1924.

20. *Young Pioneer*, November 1929, LCP.

21. *Daily Oklahoman*, 4 December 1929.

22. *New York Times*, 9 February 1918.

23. Theodore H. Von Laue, *Why Lenin? Why Stalin?*, (New York: J. B. Lippin-cott, 1971), p. 143.

24. *Daily Worker*, 3 March 1925.

25. U.S. Congress, House, Hearings before the Committee on the Judiciary House of Representatives, 68th Cong., 1st. sess., 1924, p. 60.

26. Ibid., p. 68.

27. Ibid., pp. 156–173; see Kriste Lindenmeyer, *"A Right to Childhood": The U.S. Children's Bureau and Child Welfare, 1912–46*, (Urbana: University of Illinois Press, 1997).

28. *Daily Worker*, 1 December 1924; the *Woman Patriot*, 1 January 1925.

29. See Kriste Lindenmeyer, *"A Right to Childhood,": The U.S. Children's Bureau and Child Welfare, 1912–46*, (Urbana: University of Illinois Press, 1997).

30. Letter to Kate Barnard, 21 January 1910, Department of Charities and Corrections Collections, Archives, Oklahoma Department of Libraries, Oklahoma City, Oklahoma.

31. *Harlow's Weekly*, 24 January 1925.

32. "Mustering Sentinels of the Republic," reprinted from *National Magazine*, October, 1922, Mrs. John Balch to Alice Robertson, 3 March 1923, Alice Robertson Collection, McFarlin Library, University of Tulsa; J. Stanley Lemons, *Woman Citizen, Social Feminism in the 1920s* (Urbana: University of Illinois Press, 1973), p. 219.

33. Lemon, *Woman Citizen*, pp. 123, 223.

34. Harlow, *Makers of Government in Oklahoma*, p. 63.

35. *Daughters of the American Revolution Magazine*, LCP.

36. Ibid.

37. *Harlow's Weekly*, 25 August 1923.

38. Ibid.

39. Summary of Proceedings Seventh National Convention of the American Legion Auxiliary, September 19–23, 1927. American Legion Auxiliary Collection, Archives, Oklahoma Historical Society, Oklahoma City, Oklahoma.

40. Quoted in Joan M. Jensen, "All Pink Sisters: The War Department and the Feminist Movement in the 1920s," in Lois Scharf and Joan M. Jensen, *Decades of Discontent: The Women's Movement, 1920–1940*, (Connecticut: Greenwood Press, 1983), p. 211.

41. *Harlow's Weekly*, 7 July 1923.

42. Mable Bulaud Campbell to Lola Clark Pearson, 12 April 1931, LCP.

43. Alice Yeakel to Lola Clark Pearson, 13 April 1931, LCP.

44. Mrs. G. Falck to Lola Clark Pearson, 14 April 1931, LCP.
45. Mary LaRue to Lola Clark Pearson, no date, LCP.
46. Theodora N. Youmans to Lola Clark Pearson, 12 April 1931, LCP.
47. Helen K Stuart to Lola Clark Pearson, 15 April 1931, LCP.
48. Isabel C. Patterson to Lola Clark Pearson, 14 April 1931, LCP.
49. Ethel M. White to Lola Clark Pearson, no date, LCP.
50. Julia Floyd to Lola Clark Pearson, 9 April 1931, LCP.

Representative Women, L. Prang & Co., c1870. Portraits of seven prominent figures of the suffrage and women's rights movements. Subjects include: Lucretia Mott, Grace Greenwood, Elizabeth Cady Stanton, Anne E. Dickinson, Mary Ashton Rice Livermore, Susan B Anthony, and Lydia Maria Francis Child.

Epilogue

Patriotism, Americanization programs, protection of the American family, and military preparedness were conservative themes emphasized by women's organizations in the 1920s. The DAR, the Sentinels of the Republic, the Woman's Auxiliary to the American Legion, the General Federation of Women's Clubs, and the League of Women Voters all emphasized these themes in their programs directed at educating women and immigrants to American political culture. Along with joining these organizations, more and more Oklahoma women abandoned the public sphere and assumed a more private role in securing traditional American values. The evidence for this change was not only in the increased membership in conservative organizations, but in the coverage of their activities by local newspapers.

The "Oklahoma Women in Politics" column, which initially appeared in *Harlow's Weekly* in 1920, changed to a more innocuous column entitled "Oklahoma Women" in 1923. The content of the new column focused less on women's political activity and more on the their involvement with home and family. For example, in the June 25, 1923, paper, the column announced the establishment of the Scout Mothers' Auxiliary. The stated purpose was to provide a "closer liaison between the Scouts and the home." Strengthening the tie between parents and their children was perhaps motivated by the Socialist campaign to organize school children into the Young Pioneers. At any rate, the editor related that "Wherever scout mothers' auxiliaries have been organized, the work has been materially strengthened, boys have taken more interest in their troops, scoutmasters have been inspired to do better work and to stand by the ship longer ... the hand that rocks the cradle rules the world."[1]

The "Oklahoma Women" page changed again in 1924 to a more chatty and less serious column entitled "Shoes and Ships and

Sealing Wax." The title came from Lewis Carroll's "The Walrus and the Carpenter."

> "The time has come," the Walrus said,
> "To talk of many things:
> Of shoes—and ships—and sealing-wax—
> Of cabbages—and kings—
> And why the sea is boiling hot—
> And whether pigs have wings."[2]

The meaning was clear—there was more to discuss about women than merely their new political life. In the column that debuted in the fall of 1924, Cora Miley entertained her readers with folksy ramblings about the beginning of fall in Oklahoma: "Children are again in school, women's clubs are beginning, it is harvest time in the fields." She expressed her feelings about the approaching winter and the long days ahead, and asked the challenging question, "What are we going to be doing with them?" Miley admitted that personally, "I am hoping to make home a happier place this winter. I want to change the furniture around and freshen it up a bit. I want to give more thought to the menus. I want to take more pains with my personal appearance and I want to be more interested in what concerns and interests the other members of the family and less absorbed in my own affairs." Miley also informed women that it was important for them to be involved in their club work but not to change the social, economic, or political life of the country but to learn to "take her club work seriously, for there she may improve her expression, her poise, her enunciation, her personality, as well as her mind power." Miley did write that it was important for women to vote in the 1924 presidential and congressional elections. The question was how to get women to vote. Miley surmised that only by instilling patriotism would women find interest in voting.[3]

Lola Pearson also wore the hat of newspaper columnist. In 1923 the editor of the *Oklahoma Farmer* asked Pearson to write a column that responded to readers' questions about a variety of subjects. The agreement between Pearson and the *Oklahoma Farmer* outlined the content of Pearson's material. It was important that she present to her readers timely homemaking suggestions and that topics include clothing, food, gardening, home decoration, and information on household appliances.[4] Pearson's advice to women was quite a departure from the lectures she gave to club women about their responsibilities as political citizens. Her first column as the "Farm Hawk" editor discussed the etiquette used in holding club meetings. But even though she understood that her columns were instructive toward making women good homemakers, every so often she would interject in her column advice on an issue that was not about homemaking or clubwork. Pearson offered her political observations about events in Oklahoma or the world. For example, when there was political controversy over the dismissal of the president of Oklahoma Agriculture and Mechanical College, Pearson took the opportunity to write her opinions on changing the state constitution to create a board of regents whose responsibility it would be to oversee the operations of the state's colleges and universities.[5] And in her good country style, she advised women to vote in county, state, and national elections. In June 1924 The Capper–owned *Oklahoma Farmer* merged with the *Oklahoma Farmer Stockman*, and Pearson became associate editor of the women's section in 1925.

In 1927 Pearson took over as "Good Cheer in the Home" editor when Mabel Bates Williams resigned. As the economic depression worsened in the early 1930s, the column took on new meaning as Pearson found herself in the position of providing "good cheer" to farm women who were discouraged by the uncheery economic outlook for the Oklahoma farming community.[6] Oklahoma farmers were especially hard hit in the early 1930s with low commodity prices, poor agricultural markets, and drought conditions that affected crop production. Those who suffered the most were small farmers and tenants. Many of these folks found no other recourse to their economic problems than to leave the state. Between 1935 and 1940, more than 400,000 Oklahomans emigrated to regions of the country that seemed to promise better economic prospects. The severity of the depression left the federal government with few other options than to offer government aid to those in financial need. By the end of the depression in the late 1930s, Franklin D. Roosevelt's economic recovery programs, popularly referred to as the "New Deal," ran the gamut from aid to farmers through the Agricultural Adjustment Administration to aid to musicians through the Federal Music Project. The enormous output of government resources and programs that in one way or another affected the lives of the American people met with criticism from conservatives, who continued to view federal intrusion into the economic life of the country as ultimately detrimental to the American character. Many believed that such programs as government-supported work relief, government relocation of farmers off of their lands, and government-sponsored communities would diminish individuality and the ideal that one succeeded by his own initiative and hard work. Lola Pearson reflected the conservative view in her "good cheer" column. Throughout her years as "good cheer" editor, Pearson continued to uphold her convictions that most problems in American society could be handled by individual effort with little or no government aid. As one of her readers so aptly wrote, "Dear Cheer leader: For that is what you are isn't it? You lead us to find cheer in our own circumstances, whatever they may be, and teach us to improve them if we can or bear them cheerfully if we must."[7] While Pearson offered women her "cheer," she also continued to warn Americans of a perilous future for the country if they allowed government to solve their problems. In her article in the *Oklahoma Farmer Stockman* entitled "Whither Are We Bound," Pearson puzzled over the current state of affairs in the country in 1934 and the government response. The editor wrote, "I have never before felt so much uncertainly about the tendencies of my government.... I am in a state of doubt about many things.... I just can't see how they will accomplish what to me is the aim of all government, the greatest happiness and comfort for the greatest number of people, not for the present alone but for all time." Her concern was for the welfare of the American farmer, who historically epitomized American independence. "For more than 150 years we have boasted of the independence of our farmers.... I hold that the true farmer and his family, living on even the poorest farm, is happier and more comfortable than he would be transported to a town or industrial center there to become dependent upon what day labor he could secure." Pearson directed her criticism at the Agricultural Adjustment Administration's policy of reducing the farmer's productive acreage in return for government subsidies. It did not make sense to her that reducing the cotton acreage by 15 million acres would help the tenant and sharecroppers. She estimated that more than 300,000 families would lose the farmland from which they made a living.[8] Many of Pearson's readers agreed with her assessment of the government's programs. One reader from Paducah, Texas, wrote Pearson:

> I am in hearty accord with the thoughts expressed in your editorial "Whither Are We Bound." And I must confess that I too am beset by the same uncertainty of feelings. I am wondering, groping, in doubt, and to you I am going to confess too that I still feel an occasional qualm of fear as to the final outcome, but I am not broadcasting that fact to everyone.

But I ask you what can we expect of a citizenry whose wants, like that of the pig, are spoiled by a paternalistic caretaker, and I am afraid that, in the last analysis, it bodes us not good. It will require a half-century for us to outgrow the effect of the precedent that has been established if we ever are so fortunate as to outgrow it, which I am inclined to doubt.[9]

Throughout her work in Oklahoma politics, from vice-chairman of the Oklahoma Republican party to editor of the *Oklahoma Farmer Stockman*, Lola Clark Pearson promoted her conservative view for American society. There were many Oklahoma women who held Pearson's beliefs. But there were also many women whose politics were at the other end of the political spectrum. Regardless of their political ideology, in the early 1920s most women continued to promote progressive legislation that would benefit women and children. But their progressivism began to fade as the country turned more conservative by mid-decade. One of the primary reasons for this shift was women's concern for the welfare of the American family and their concern for the deterioration of traditional American values brought on by the changing economy of the 1920s. By 1930, most conservative women were no longer taking an active role in the political life of the country. Pearson's was perhaps one of the few voices that continued to question the role of government in American life. As the pendulum swings, however, so too the political convictions of the American people. As the economic depression worsened throughout the 1930s, political activists, men and women, once again suggested that other government systems, like socialism, could offer solutions to the country's economic problems not provided by Capitalism. In many ways, the 1930s were the antithesis of the 1920s. The politics of Oklahomans fell in line accordingly.

NOTES

1. *Harlow's Weekly*, 25 June 1923.
2. Lewis Carroll, "The Walrus and the Carpenter," in *Through the Looking Glass and What Alice Found There*, 1872.
3. *Harlow's Weekly*, 6 September 1924.
4. Ida Migliario to Lola Clark Pearson, 4 December 1923, Lola Clark Pearson Collection, Western History Archive, University of Oklahoma. Hereafter cited LCP.
5. *Oklahoma Farmer*, 25 June 1923.

6. *The Story of the Farmer-Stockman*, (Oklahoma City, 1956), p. 5.
7. Olive P. Jolly to Lola Clark Pearson, 25 January 1934, LCP.
8. The *Oklahoma Farmer Stockman*, 15 April 1934.
9. M. C. Young to Lola Clark Pearson, 18 April 1934, LCP.

Index

175

Masons 70, 91, 127, 129, 130, 133, 144, 150
Matron's Magazine, The 6
McColgin, Bessie 55, 67
McColgin, Grant 67
McCormick, Ruth Hanna 36
McDougal, D. A. 61
McDougal, Myrtle Archer 35, 45, 48, 49, 50, 61, 62, 63, 68, 144
McGraw, James J. 38, 64, 91, 165
McKinley, Pres. Wm. 100, 101
McVean, Margaret 82
Merrie Wives, The 6
Mertz, Dora 23
Miley, Cora 89, 170
Minerva Home 98
Minimum Wage 47, 84
Minnesota Federation of Women's Clubs 162
Mitchell, Edith 85, 142
Mother Jones 19
Muskogee Klan No. 16 138
Nagle, Mrs. Patrick S. 152
Nagle, Patrick S. 25, 29, 151, 152
National American Woman Suffrage Association 1, 40, 73, 91. *See also* NAW-
     SA
National Association for the Advancement of Colored People 78
National Association of Colored Women 58, 60, 78
National Association Opposed to Woman Suffrage 103
National Child Labor Committee 26, 113, 154
National Consumers' League 41, 113
National Democrat Committee 156
National Executive Committee of the Republican party 156
National Law and Order League 143
National League of Liberty 143
National Organization of Federated Clubs 163
National Socialist Party 28
National Suffrage Convention 17
National Suffrage Organization 4
National Woman's Party 7, 40, 47, 69, 77, 78, 79, 81, 82, 84, 85, 90, 92, 93,
     112, v
National Women's Democrat Club 65
National Women's Trade Union League 41, 156
NAWSA 1, 74, 77, 78, 91. *See also* National American Woman Suffrage As-
     sociation
Neighbors of Woodcraft 134

Other Books from Horse Creek Publications

Schrems, Suzanne H., *Uncommon Women, Unmarked Trails: The Courageous Journey of Catholic Missionary Sisters In Frontier Montana*. Horse Creek Publications, Inc. 2003

Maddux, Vernon R., *In Dull Knife's Wake: The True Story of the Northern Cheyenne Exodus of 1878*, Horse Creek Publications, 2003.

Del Bene, Terry A., *Donner Party Cookbook*, Horse Creek Publications, 2003.

Visit the Horse Creek web site at:
www.HorseCreekPublications.com